Compulsive Buying

Compulsive Buying

Consumer Traits, Self-Regulation, and Marketing Ethics

Trevor A. Smith and Kenroy C. Wedderburn

LEXINGTON BOOKS
Lanham • Boulder • New York • London

Short dedication—14/16

Lengthy dedication—Text size

Bring down to align with top of copyright.

Published by Lexington Books
An imprint of The Rowman & Littlefield Publishing Group, Inc.
4501 Forbes Boulevard, Suite 200, Lanham, Maryland 20706
www.rowman.com

86-90 Paul Street, London EC2A 4NE

British Library Cataloguing in Publication Information Available

Library of Congress Cataloging-in-Publication Data

Names: Smith, Trevor A., 1958- author. | Wedderburn, Kenroy C., 1967- author.
Title: Compulsive buying : consumer traits, self-regulation, and marketing ethics / Trevor A. Smith and Kenroy C. Wedderburn.
Description: Lanham : Lexington Books, [2022] | Includes bibliographical references and index.
Identifiers: LCCN 2021038897 (print) | LCCN 2021038898 (ebook) | ISBN 9781793645739 (cloth) | ISBN 9781793645753 (paper) | ISBN 9781793645746 (epub)
Subjects: LCSH: Compulsive shopping. | Shopping—Psychological aspects.
Classification: LCC RC569.5.S56 S65 2022 (print) | LCC RC569.5.S56 (ebook) | DDC 616.85/84—dc23
LC record available at https://lccn.loc.gov/2021038897
LC ebook record available at https://lccn.loc.gov/2021038898

Contents

Acknowledgments

This book is built on the prior research in the area of compulsive buying. It also embodies years of conversations that we have had with colleagues, friends, and family members on the pervasive topic of shopping. The book has therefore benefitted from both the scholarly literature and the rich exchanges we have had with people on their shopping experiences. We are certainly grateful for the collective wisdom gained from the potpourri of ideas. Although the book is rich with inputs from so many people, there are a few individuals who we must mention by name for special thank you. In particular, Roshelle Lewis who provided research assistance, doing the literature search, and engaging us in the Theory of Self-Regulation of which she felt was the quintessential theory for explaining the curtailment of addictive behaviours. To Maxine McDonnough, who took us to editing school through scrupulous care and untiring pursuit to make sure that our manuscript was easily readable and understandable. To Henry Lewis, who was up many times while we were asleep reading our chapters and providing very insightful comments on how we could improve the manuscript. To Trevaughn Smith, who served as graphics man on the book and made sure that our schemas were mean and clean. To Travis Smith, who quietly provided computer support and handled computer glitches and technical problems during the preparation of the book. Last but not least, we especially thank you for reading *Compulsive Buying: The Role of Consumer Traits, Self-Regulation, and Marketing Ethic*s, a book which we hope you will find useful for explicating the nuances of compulsive buying behaviour.

Introduction

Shopping is a basic activity that is encouraged by the state as consumer spending is one of the key drivers of macroeconomic performance. This is a talking point among political interest groups, and you will always hear that sales are up or down in any given year, making shopping a barometer for economic performance and a desirable and acceptable activity for citizens to engage in.

Shopping is a problem for compulsive buyers who are people who buy excessively, making purchases that they may not need and can ill afford to buy. Many people, however, shop to satisfy materialistic tendencies, i.e., loving material possessions, and are not classified as compulsive buyers. Still, compulsive buyers are usually materialistic, even though not all materialism is related to compulsive buying.

Materialism, in a broad sense, can be seen as a value system and not a buying disorder. A person who is materialistic uses material goods and things as a part of their success or status or as a means of comparing themselves with others. Many people who are not materialistic may just like to shop, and some will go to the mall when they are feeling depressed or are in a low mood and shop just to soothe their moods. However, what might have started out as an innocent and pleasurable activity of retail therapy can lead to shopping addiction and end up in buyer's remorse and money problems.

The psychology of consumer shopping is complex with many dimensions, not least of which is compulsive buying which is the subject of this book. In addressing this difficult problem, the book presents an integrative discourse on compulsive buying and seeks to assess addictive buying behaviour from the standpoint of the customer who buys compulsively and the outlook of the firm whose marketing activities are geared towards compulsive and excessive consumption, i.e., through advertising and promotion, the marketer will trig-

1

ger the urge in the shopper to engage in excessive buying so that marketing can satisfy its sales targets.

This introductory chapter will continue with a brief discourse on the consumer buying process aimed at providing insights on the fundamentals of buying. The distinction is made between the customer who purchases the goods and the consumer who uses these goods—both parties being integral to the buying process. An introduction to compulsive buying behaviour is next presented followed by a few pointers on the rationale and importance of this book. Through a preliminary assessment of buying behaviour, the chapter identifies key demographic variables such as gender and age that are associated with compulsive buying. The two schools of personality traits that gave methodological guidance to the architecture of this book are also discussed in the chapter. In addition, the roles of consumer trait, self-regulation and marketing ethics in compulsive buying behaviour are then discussed in setting the stage for the integrative framework that underlies this book. The chapter concludes with a guide on the organization of the manuscript, a checklist of lessons learnt, and a synopsis of the chapters.

THE CONSUMER BUYING PROCESS

Buying is a routine process and a normal way of advancing the day to day lives of consumers. People buy goods and services to satisfy both basic needs, e.g., food, clothing and shelter, and acquired needs, e.g., achievement, affiliation, and power. Buying is, therefore, a necessary activity of modern life. The activity of buying has become very challenging with more things to buy and less money to make the purchases. A good buy is, therefore, a planned and deliberate behaviour that is regulated through proper budgeting.

Shoppers are now making lots of purchases online, buying unwanted goods, and returning goods have become a hassle with online shopping. Returning of goods purchased online usually involves return post and most people are too lazy or simply cannot be bothered to do the return. These unwanted goods are creating space issues within homes and, ultimately, ending up in landfills.

The activity of buying is impacted by factors that are both external and internal to the consumer. These external factors include television advertising and in-store stimuli while internal factors include moods, attitudes, and consumer traits.

Smith (2019) suggests that buying from the customer perspective is a participatory process, which, in the purest sense, can only take place when the customer has established the need, has the intention to buy and can justifiably afford to make the purchase. Hence, for Smith (2019), the salesman will sell, and the customer will acquire, but the act of buying requires the intersection of three states—need, intention, and affordability. The buying process is integrative and has three main touchpoints—search, purchase, and after-sales service (Gensler et al. 2012). The search and purchase are done by the buyer and the after-sales service is done by the seller.

The firm is more focused on the act of selling to the consumer rather than on customer buying. Selling is seen as a more proactive way to generate revenues than buying. After all, buying falls squarely in the hands of the customer while selling is the remit of the firm. Moreover, selling involves the persuasion of the customer to buy within the firm's time frame (e.g., to meet monthly sales targets) while buying is more geared at making the purchase within the time line of the customer. Thus, selling is expected to better influence the frequency and timeliness of cash flows that are required by the business to keep afloat. However, buying on the part of the customer, being a voluntary process, is expected to be a better driver of customer loyalty than selling. This is certainly the case in the life insurance industry where *hard-sell,* i.e., selling through high-pressured sales techniques, is attributed to high levels of lapsed policies while *soft-sell* which is giving the customer the opportunity to buy based on need, intention, and affordability is expected to keep the customers loyal and maintain their policies on the books (Smith 2019).

CUSTOMER VERSUS CONSUMER

The discourse on compulsive buying must first make the distinction between customers and consumers. This distinction is necessary to properly identify where the compulsion lies—customer, consumer or both. The customer is the buyer of goods, i.e, the individual or entity who makes the purchase while the consumer is the end-user (individual or entity) who consumes the purchased goods. Many consumers, such as children, who may not be directly involved in the purchase and are therefore not customers, may still have a lot of influence on the customers, who are most likely their parents. Any study on compulsive buying, therefore, must take both customer and consumer into consideration as the customer plays the direct role in the buying process while the consumer plays the indirect. Moreover, the customer or purchaser regularly plays a dual role in the buying process as he/she is often a consumer of the goods and services purchased.

INTRODUCTION TO COMPULSIVE BUYING BEHAVIOUR

Compulsive buying is described as an unhealthy preoccupation with shopping and buying excesses that lead to distress, impairments, and other adverse consequences (Black 2007; Müller et al. 2019). It is characterized by an irresistible-uncontrollable urge and known to cause obsession with shopping thereby creating anxiety when not shopping. Other consequences of compulsive buying include the purchase of unnecessary or unwanted goods, expensive purchases and time-consuming retail activities. People with this predisposition are usually insecure, have low self-esteem with mood problems, and have difficulties to control shopping impulses. With these problems, many people affected by the condition will naturally have problems with personal, family, and professional lives.

The term compulsive buying is often used interchangeably with terms such as compulsive purchasing, compulsive shopping, and compulsive spending (Nataraajan and Goff 1992). The scientific term for this disorder is oniomania, and other alternative descriptors used are shopping addiction and pathological buying (Harnish, Bridges and Karelitz 2017). In this book, for the most part, the term compulsive buying will be used, and this is the term most frequently used in the existing literature.

When we think of an addiction, what typically comes to mind is substance abuse and not compulsive buying. Compulsive buying was originally described by Emil Kraepelin, a German psychiatrist, in 1924, but little interest was taken in the condition until the 1990s (Black 2007). This addictive condition is not listed in the DSM-5 of the American Psychiatric Association or the ICD-10 of the World Health Organization (Granero et al. 2016). This therefore suggests that the shopping behaviour may not be easily classified or diagnosed. It is not clear whether compulsive buying is an impulse control disorder or an addictive disorder (Harnish et al. 2017). This need for clarification is perhaps the reason why the American Psychiatric Association did not include compulsive buying in the DSM-5 as other similar conditions such as gambling disorder have been included. Compulsive buying is also viewed by marketers as a stimulus-response shopping problem that causes the shopper to hastily respond to advertising and promotional cues. As such, this behaviour is likened to impulsive buying and seen as a more severe case of an impulsive consumption (Verplanken and Sato 2011).

Some people have argued that compulsive buying should not be seen as a disorder at all and that this is just a trend to medicalize behavioural problems. Nonetheless, there is psychiatric claim that compulsive buying may be treated successfully with antidepressant drugs (McElroy et al. 1994; Mestel 1994). Thus, from a clinical perspective, compulsive buying is treated as a psychiatric disorder but more recently, there have been calls for the problem to be treated as a materialistic tendency that causes uncontrolled buying behaviour (Kasser and Kanner 2004). This latter view accords with the position of the marketers. Besides, there is overwhelming evidence of an association between materialism and compulsive buying behaviour (Pirog and Roberts 2007). This multidisciplinary issue of compulsive buying has been explored in the areas of psychiatry, psychology, and behavioural marketing because of its widespread impact on the buying population.

Compulsive buyers are those individuals with a dopamine-fuelled shopping addiction who get the rush of adrenalin when making a purchase. These people live to shop, and shopping may even be viewed as a companion by many of them. In extreme cases, some would say that shopping is their life or there would be no life without shopping. No doubt, shopping controls these individuals. The behaviour of compulsive buying is developed through self-talking that leads to a preoccupation with shopping. This shopping experience comes with an intense involvement and the process of shopping is completed with a purchase and often followed with a sense of disappointment in oneself. During this process, the compulsive buyers go through endorphin highs and guilt-ridden lows creating in the buyer mixed feelings of excitement and disappointment.

Compulsive buying is prevalent among the general shopping public with reported cases as high as 16.4 percent in the United Kingdom (Maccarrone-Eaglen and Schofield 2017), 29.1 percent in China (He et al. 2018) and worldwide prevalence estimated at 1 percent to 8 percent (Weinstein et al. 2016). Other estimates have indicated that the prevalence rate of compulsive buyers could range between 1 percent and 10 percent in Western developed economies (Dittmar 2005).

The compulsive buyer rarely uses cash as it is psychologically more painful to spend with cash when compared with digital spending. This excessive spending is usually a symptom of something much deeper in the psychological antecedence of the buyer. That said, compulsive buying is associated with genetics and there is evidence to suggest that it runs in families (Black 2012). This addictive behaviour is believed to have comorbidities with a number of other conditions. These include depression, anxiety and hoarding (Hayward and Coles 2009; Heshmat 2018), bipolar disorder (Kesebir et al. 2012), eating disorder (Lejoyeux and Weinstein 2010), and other impulse control disorders (Hagedorn 2009; Nicoli de Mattos et al. 2016; Lejoyeux and Weinstein 2010). More generally, these compulsive buyers are usually troubled with buying anxiety, have addictive buying problems and characteristically shop on impulse, leading to acquisition of expensive and often unwanted products.

Women and Compulsive Buying

This trait of compulsive buying is overrepresented among women shoppers (Zadka and Olajossy 2016). Hence, many studies in this area are focused on women (Rajesh 2019). These studies have shown that the prevalence rate of women compulsive buyers ranges from a low of 74 percent (Hanley and Wilhelm 1992) to a high of 93 percent (Black et al. 1998). Another study has reported the incidence of women with an average of 90 percent compared with men at 10 percent (Dittmar 2005). These findings on gender are quite startling and suggest that women are much more susceptible to compulsive buying habits than men.

Age, Gender, and Compulsive Buying

Prior research has demonstrated that age is negatively correlated with compulsive buying behaviour (Achtziger et al. 2015; d'Astous 1990; Dittmar 2005; Magee 1994). This means that younger people are more likely to be compulsive buyers than older people. In explaining the relationship between age and compulsive buying behaviour, Myers (2000) found that compulsive buying is associated with materialism and younger people tend to be more materialistic than their older counterparts. Achtziger et al. (2015) found that gender was effective in predicting compulsive buying, and again, women were more prone than men to this behaviour. However, while it can be concluded that women in the general population are far more compulsive buyers than men, the stark difference in compulsive buying behaviour of females compared with males may not be as wide among teenagers and younger adults (Dittmar 2005). These shifting indicators on age, gender, and compulsive buying need to be researched further for more insights on buying in the twenty-first century.

THE TWO SCHOOLS OF PERSONALITY TRAITS

Consumer personality is a complex phenomenon but can be studied and better understood through personality trait theories of which there are two influential schools of thought. The first school believes that all individuals have the same set of personality traits and individual differences are explained by the degree to which these traits are displayed in one individual versus another. The second school believes that individual difference is explained through trait combination in which everyone has a specific set of personality traits, and not all traits, with everyone having these traits uniquely combined making one individual characteristically different from another.

The application of consumer trait in predicting compulsive buying that was done in this undertaking is predicated on the first school and so the sample of shoppers studied were assumed to have all the consumer traits depicted in the model with individual differences accounting for very low to very high representation of each trait. For example, shoppers self-reporting on the consumer trait of impulsiveness and assess themselves as not being impulsive would rate themselves at 1, indicating a very low level of impulsiveness on a Likert scale ranging from 1 to 5. Conversely, those shoppers who rate themselves as highly impulsive would rate themselves at 5. In addition, shoppers who rate themselves as being neither highly impulsive nor impulsive at all would rate themselves somewhere in the middle between 1 and 5.

THE ROLE OF CONSUMER
TRAITS IN COMPULSIVE BUYING BEHAVIOUR

There are many consumer predispositions that could influence the phenomenon of compulsive buying. These predispositions would include attitudes, moods, motivation, and personality traits that are internal to the consumer. Similarly, there are external conditions (e.g., family, society and culture) and situational context (e.g., loss of job or death of love ones) that could influence this behaviour. Compulsive buying is therefore a very complex behaviour as it could be triggered by so many consumer traits, conditions, and situations which themselves could operate either singly or in combination, thus making the triggers of compulsive behaviour very confounding and rendering any scientific explanation of this behaviour to be work-in-progress at best. That said, there is consensus in the existing research which suggests that consumer personality traits provide at least a part of the explanation for buying behavioural outcomes such as brand loyalty (Smith 2015), gambling activities (Fang and Mowen 2009), credit card misuse (Pirog and Roberts 2007), and negative consumption-based emotions (Mooradian and Olver 1997). Compulsive buying behaviour is viewed as a consumer trait as it represents an enduring consumption-based predisposition (Mowen 2000). More precisely, it can be described as a surface level personality trait. The trait approach was therefore utilized in this undertaking in an attempt to explain compulsive buying and predict this negative buying behaviour from a set of consumption traits.

This approach was found to be a best fit for addressing this buyer behavioural problem for several reasons. First, individual differences, which make up personality traits, account for a significant portion of the variability in consumer consumption (Mowen 2000). This means that our personalities explain a large portion of the reasons as to how and why we consume. Second, many consumer predispositions, including compulsive buying, are trait-like in nature and can therefore be modelled using trait theories for a good fit. For example, to have a vanity predisposition or a negative attitude to status consumption are trait-like constructs[1] which could be modelled using the Meta-theoretic Model of Motivation and Personality for predicting compulsive buying. See Mowen (2000) on this theory.

THE ROLE OF SELF-REGULATION
IN COMPULSIVE BUYING BEHAVIOUR

Self-regulation is a human behavioural process that leads to positive outcomes on effective execution. This internal process is essential for regulating and controlling human behaviour. People are able to govern their thoughts, feelings, emotions and shopping behaviour through self-regulation. It is expected, therefore, that an effective regulation of self will lead to more favourable behavioural outcomes and a more fulfilling life (Baumeister and Vohs 2018). That said, almost all personal problems that people experience are associated with the failure to self-regulate (Vohs and Baumeister 2016).

Self-regulation is administered through a feedback loop for consciously controlling thoughts and behaviour towards the attainment of goals or outcomes (Baumeister et al. 2006). Notably, this process is fundamental to the control of all human behaviour and obviously not specific to compulsive buying. However, it is believed that through the self-regulation process, consumers can better control this addictive behaviour of buying compulsively.

This book will address the role of self-regulation in mitigating compulsive buying behaviour. It will present a theoretical framework for explaining the epistemology of the self-regulatory process and highlight the prior research that gave rise to this association between self-regulation and compulsive buying.

THE ROLE OF MARKETING
ETHICS IN COMPULSIVE BUYING BEHAVIOUR

The primary aim of marketing is to uncover the needs of the customer and make a profit by serving and satisfying these needs. This practice has raised questions on the ethics of the marketing function and whether it is designed to exploit the vulnerability of customers that is presented through their physical and psychological needs. In response to this ethical dilemma, the socially responsible firm pursues ethical practices in service to its customers. Thus, marketing ethics is an embodiment of the guiding principles of the firm for carrying out the marketing activities responsibly.

Ethics in marketing is a controversial topic since there is always the conflict between making money and being socially responsible. Nonetheless, the socially responsible firm is not only seeking to make profits but also seeks to ensure that marketing is practiced fairly and provides societal benefits for assisting vulnerable groups (Mikolajczak-Degrauwe and Brengman 2014). That said, marketing ethics have not gone far enough in addressing the vulnerability of consumers with problems such as compulsive buying behaviour. Moreover, the marketer is an active partner in the psychological problems that are experienced by compulsive buyers since marketing is designed to create the urge in the customer, through advertising and promotion, thus triggering the customer to make the purchase and even buying compulsively.

This book will address the ethical considerations in marketing to compulsive buyers and will provide guidelines to the firm for addressing this problem. These guidelines include a template for identifying compulsive buyers and a programme of ethical readiness for treating with these buyers.

RATIONALE AND IMPORTANCE OF THIS BOOK

Compulsive buying behaviour will often result in personal problems, financial hardship and dysfunctional families. These consequences provide a good reason for the study of this buying behaviour. Buying abuse is also a matter of public policy as the State has, among its responsibilities, the challenging task of overseeing the welfare and wellbeing of citizens. Another good reason for studying compulsive buying behaviour, therefore, is to provide guidance to policymakers for helping this vulnerable group.

The book is important to this stream of work as it provides an integrative and contemporary discourse on the problem of compulsive buying—a worrying phenomenon that continues to be pervasive among the wider buying population. The use of the consumer traits model for predicting and explaining compulsive buying behaviour is also quite significant as personality traits remain underutilized in explaining consumer behaviour (Mowen 2000)—compulsive buying being entrenched within the discipline of consumer behaviour. Moreover, the association of self-regulation and marketing ethics with compulsive buying is also significant as little is known of these linkages.

A distinctive feature of the project is that the book does not only focus on the compulsivity of the individual but also addresses the firm vis-à-vis ethical considerations that marketers could utilize in marketing goods and services to compulsive buyers.

There is a reasonable number of academic articles that have given coverage to this subject of compulsive buying. However, only a few books have been written in this area. Books are therefore needed for expanded coverage, particularly for integrative knowledge on the psychological drivers of the behaviour, the self-fix strategies for dealing with the condition and the social responsibility of business for dealing with this problem. After all, compulsive buying is a shopping problem, and the literature has not gone far enough in addressing the contribution of the firm to this buying behaviour or how the firm could assist in mitigating this societal problem. This book has addressed the gap through an integrative framework that combines the consumer trait drivers for predicting compulsive buying, the self-regulation process for controlling the behaviour and the ethical considerations in marketing to this vulnerable group. It is hoped that through this integrative framework a more holistic approach can be found for addressing this problem.

HOW IS THE BOOK ORGANIZED?

The book is organized through an integrative framework that is depicted in Figure I.1.

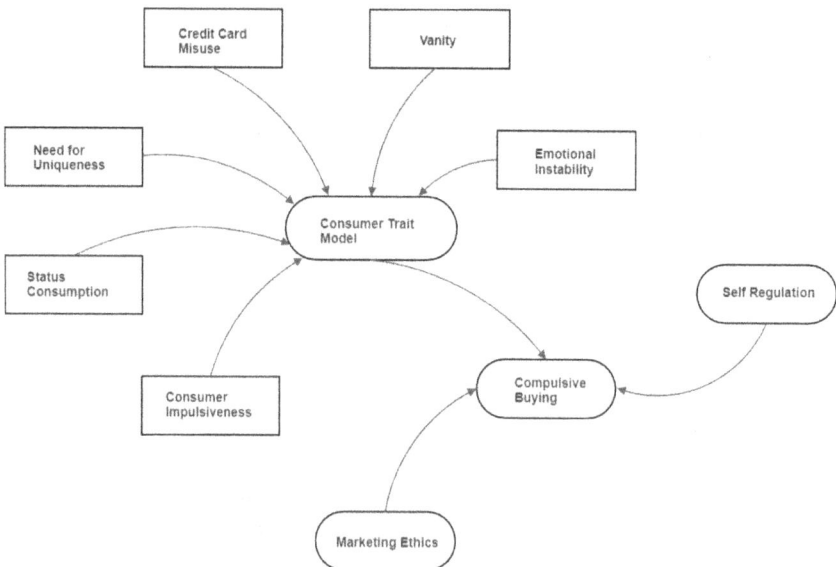

Figure I.1.   Integrative Framework on Compulsive Buying and Related Constructs.
Created by the authors.

This integrative framework is developed over the following chapters:

- Introduction
- Chapter 1: Compulsive Buying Behaviour
- Chapter 2: Personality, Personality Traits, and Consumer Traits
- Chapter 3: A Consumer Trait Model for Predicting Compulsive Buying
- Chapter 4: The Influence of the Credit Card on Compulsive Buying
- Chapter 5: Self-Regulating Compulsive Buying Behaviour
- Chapter 6: The Ethical Considerations in Marketing to Compulsive Buyers
- Conclusion

WHO SHOULD READ THIS BOOK?

The primary market for this work consists of students who are pursuing their programme of study in business schools and in the social sciences. This will be particularly suited to students taking courses in marketing, consumer behaviour, and psychology. The book can be used as prescribed reading in business management programmes and targeted at both the undergraduate and graduate levels (MBA and other graduate programmes). It could also be used as recommended reading for students studying behavioural sciences to advance the understanding of consumer traits, self-regulation, and marketing ethics. The book is targeted at an international audience and is not intended to be country specific.

The book is also targeted at researchers who are undertaking a stream of work in marketing, consumer behaviour, and psychology. Nonetheless, the manuscript is written in easily understood language, utilizing simple examples and scenarios, to be consumed by a wide cross-section of readers yet grounded in scholarship, to benefit academics thus utilizing theories and other epistemological underpinnings of the scholarly discourse.

Other audiences such as marketing professionals and business leaders could benefit from the discourse in general and on the ethical considerations in marketing goods and services to compulsive buyers, more specifically. The general public should also find interest in this book as it advances an understanding of the role of consumer traits in compulsive buying behaviour and the self-regulation of this behaviour towards better buying habits.

Synopsis of Chapters

The book consists of a set of related topics on compulsive buying behaviour.

Introduction—The introduction sets the stage for the book by discussing the fundamentals of buying, introducing compulsive buying behaviour, enunciating the importance of the work, and briefly discussing the key concepts that are relevant to the architecture of the book. An integrative framework of the book was presented and a brief overview of each of the key components of study—compulsive buying, consumer trait model, self-regulation and marketing ethics were highlighted.

Chapter 1: Compulsive Buying Behaviour—This chapter discusses some of the various strands of research on the etiology of compulsive buying. It presents a brief overview of some of the disorders that are relevant to the discussion on compulsive buying. These include obsessive-compulsive disorder, impulse control disorder, and mood disorders. The marketing perspective on classifying compulsive buying as a stimulus-response shopping problem that resembles impulsive buying was also introduced. Theories of OCD, social cognition, conspicuous consumption, and leisure class were also explored for a triangulated understanding of compulsive buying behaviour.

Chapter 2: Personality, Personality Traits, and Consumer Traits—This chapter addresses the context for relating personality traits to compulsive buying making reference to the equivalence between basic personality traits and consumer traits. It traces the early research on basic personality traits such as the seminal work of Allport and Odbert and the Big 5 Personality Typology. It also addresses the contemporary thinking on personality traits such as Mowen (2000) and Mowen and Spears (1999). The chapter then sets the stage for developing a predictive model for relating consumer traits to compulsive buying through a call for further research by Mowen (2000) on the exploration of personality traits in consumer behaviour.

Chapter 3: A Consumer Trait Model for Predicting Compulsive Buying— This chapter presents the development and testing of an empirical model that utilized survey data and structural equations modelling, for predicting compulsive buying from a set of consumer traits. This model was quite successful in predicting the pathological shopping behaviour as over 40 percent of the manifestation of compulsive buying was explained by six traits. Notably, consumer impulsiveness, credit card misuse, vanity, and emotional instability were found to be positive drivers of compulsive buying. However, contrary to expectations, no evidence was found for associations between status consumption or need for uniqueness and compulsive buying.

Chapter 4: The Influence of the Credit Card on Compulsive Buying—This chapter discusses the influence of the credit card on compulsive buying behaviour. It was empirically determined in the previous chapter that credit card misuse was the number one driver of this addictive behaviour and so the credit card was singled out for special treatment among the drivers of compulsive buying. The chapter further explores this relationship between the credit card and compulsive buying and discusses the connection between marketing of the credit card by the issuer and its misuse by the cardholder. The prior research on the link between credit card and compulsive buying and the insights drawn from the prior research are also discussed in this chapter.

Chapter 5: Self-Regulating Compulsive Buying Behaviour—This chapter addresses self-regulation in general terms while making the connection with compulsive buying behaviour. It is felt that a general understanding of self-regulation could help the compulsive buyer to exercise the necessary control for curbing this behaviour. The chapter begins with a background on self-regulation, makes reference to behavioural versus emotional self-regulation, and explains the real-world context that gives rise to the association between self-regulation and compulsive buying. The chapter also presents a conceptual model that was developed by the authors of this book, for explaining the linkages between self-regulation and compulsive buying behaviour. In addition, strategies for self-regulating consumer traits that drive compulsive buying behaviour are also discussed.

Chapter 6: The Ethical Considerations in Marketing to Compulsive Buyers—The authors introduced a rationale for the discourse on ethical considerations in marketing to compulsive buyers. This chapter includes a brief discussion on ethics in marketing with highlights on the marketing mix and possible dilemmas faced by marketing managers. These discussions also addressed marketing and utilitarianism and presented the philosophical argument that marketing actions are in pursuit of the *greater good* and may therefore be in conflict with service to smaller and vulnerable groups. Marketing management considerations in providing for compulsive buyers are discussed and a template for identifying compulsive buyers and tendencies is included. Central to the discussions in the chapter is the marketing to compulsive buyers on ethical grounds. In this context, marketing ethics is discussed vis-a-vis marketing to consumers with compulsive buying traits and marketing to vulnerable segments such as women, children, and teenagers who are prone to compulsive buying tendencies. These discussions are concluded with a framework that utilized prompting questions for assessing the ethical readiness of the firm for treating with customers who are prone to compulsive buying behaviour and tendencies.

Conclusion—The conclusion presents a brief size-up of the book and the lessons learnt from this undertaking. In short, the book commenced with a discourse on compulsive buying behaviour, discussed the role of personality and consumer traits in addictive shopping, developed and tested a model for predicting compulsive buying and highlighted the pivotal role of the credit card in this shopping behaviour. In addition, the book discussed self-regulation as the approach for mitigating compulsive buying, ethical considerations in marketing to these troubled buyers, and lessons learnt from the integrative study of compulsive buying behaviour.

LESSONS LEARNT

The lessons learnt are as follows.

1. People who are likely to buy compulsively can reasonably be identified from a set of related consumer traits.
2. The consumer traits of consumer impulsiveness, credit card misuse, vanity, and emotional instability are key drivers of compulsive buying behaviour.
3. Credit card misuse is the number one driver of compulsive buying behaviour.
4. The average shopper has low levels of the traits of impulsiveness, credit card misuse, emotional instability and compulsive buying and moderate levels of the vanity trait.
5. Shoppers with compulsive buying tendencies are likely to buy compulsively and fully fledged compulsive buyers will engage in addictive shopping even when they do not have the consumer trait tendencies.
6. Compulsive buying behaviour can be controlled by consumers through a process of self-regulation.
7. There are ethical considerations in marketing to compulsive buyers.

A FINAL NOTE

The predisposition of compulsive buying has severe implications for both the affected individuals and the wider society. Thus, an understanding of this phenomenon is a first step in helping those affected to stem this problem. This book utilized an integrative approach to predict, explain, and mitigate compulsive buying vis-à-vis consumer personality traits, consumer personality modelling, credit card misuse, self-regulation, and ethical considerations for marketers. It is hoped that this practical and systematic approach to the problem of compulsive buying will provide further understanding of this complex behaviour.

NOTE

1. A construct is a set of variables which taken together gives an overall meaning to the variable. For example, the construct of neuroticism consists of the variables 1. moodier than others, 2. overemotional, 3. easily irritated, and 4. up and down moods.

Chapter One

Compulsive Buying Behaviour

INTRODUCTION

This chapter highlights some of the various strands of research on the etiology of compulsive buying and notes the sometimes conflicting conclusions from some of the research. It is also of significance that there is no agreement among researchers on a common definition or a classification of the disorder, and there is no agreement on whether the disorder should be classified as a type of obsessive-compulsive disorder, impulse control disorder, mood disorder or addictive disorder. This chapter explains the differences among these disorders. There is also the perspective among marketers that compulsive buying may be a stimulus-response shopping problem that resembles impulsive buying.

The typical consumer makes purchases after assessing and making decisions about the utility and value of the items. However, this is not the case with compulsive buyers as these individuals get out of control with their purchases. And like substance abuse, the victims display an inability to control the overwhelming urges and participate in the abusive activities even to the detriment of their health. Similarly, victims of compulsive buying behaviour display an inability to control the urges to make purchases even when they do not need the items or cannot afford to make the purchases (Granero et al. 2016; Dittmar 2005). Thus, compulsive buying in this work is also addressed from both the perspectives of a mental health disorder and stimulus-response shopping behaviour.

People displaying compulsive buying disorder are subjected to increasing, excessive urges to shop, and these urges are not assuaged unless the purchases are made (Black 2007). Even though compulsive buyers, for the most part, make purchases for themselves, there is high incidence of them also purchasing items for family and friends (Workman and Paper 2010). This may indicate that the recipients of these consumer items may not be aware of the disorder present in the compulsive buyer, as accepting the items may serve as encouragement for the behaviour. Hence, both customers and consumers are integral to the compulsive buying process. The consequences of the addictive behaviour include a range of personal (including guilt and shame), relationship (including destruction of family, work and other relationships), and financial (including credit card abuse and bankruptcy) problems. Attempts to stop the abusive behaviours by the abusers typically fail (Granero et al. 2016).

The affliction has also been proven to have comorbidity with other illnesses like depression, anxiety, and hoarding (Hayward and Coles 2009; Heshmat 2018), bipolar disorder (Kesebir, İşitmez and Gündoğar 2012), eating disorder (Lejoyeux and Weinstein 2010), and, generally, with other impulse control disorders (Hagedorn 2009; Nicoli de Mattos et al. 2016; Lejoyeux and Weinstein 2010). Comorbidity indicates that the illness coexists with other disorders, whereby in some cases they have similar antecedents and in other cases one or more have causal relationships with others. This indicates the spiral of suffering that the victim of compulsive buying may encounter.

Compulsive buying, which was given the name oniomania, has been compared to other impulse disorders like pyromania (inability to resist the urge to directly start fires) and kleptomania (inability to resist the urge to steal). The disorder has also been compared with other addictive behaviours such as obsessive-compulsive disorder, gambling and mood disorders in this chapter. Goldsmith and McElroy (2000) suggested three criteria that could be used to diagnose whether a person is afflicted with compulsive buying disorder.

1. The frequent preoccupation with excessive shopping.
2. The behaviour causing distress and disrupting other aspects of the individual's personal, social, and financial life.
3. The shopping does not only occur during periods of mania or hyomania.

Similarly, Kuzma and Black (2006) provided a set of clinical signs that are typical of persons experiencing the compulsive buying disorder (p. 28).

- Onset in late adolescence to early adulthood
- Behaviours include shopping frequently, spending inappropriately, and fantasizing about future purchases
- Psychiatric comorbidity (mood disorders, substance abuse, eating disorders) is common among patients and first-degree relatives
- Chronic symptoms wax and wane, with widely varying severity

- Irresistible urges triggering spending
- Shopping is intensely exciting, with fleeting feelings of happiness and power
- Feelings of distress and guilt developing after shopping—patients often hide purchases
- Patients may be in denial or feel embarrassed to disclose symptoms

Other issues connected with compulsive buying such as buyer's high, shopping emotions, guilt and remorse along with the *pain of paying* are also discussed in the chapter.

Black (2012) believed that addictive behaviours such as compulsive buying may have its origin during childhood. If at a vulnerable stage of a child's development there is exposure to stressful situations this may significantly diminish the child's ability to be resilient to similar stressors later as an adult. Increased intensity and frequency of these stressors would only make the situation worse, and in such cases these children, on becoming adults, would be more susceptible to substance or behaviour addictions as their fight/flight response mechanism. Black (2012) suggested that the family, as the unique institution whose culture and environment plays a great role in the development of children, serve to foster these disorders. The fact that the same environment impacts all the children in the same family may be the reason why certain classes of disorders seem to run in families. Black (2007) noted that people displaying compulsive buying typically have close family members displaying symptoms of either behaviour or substance abuse disorders. In a child's formative years, the norms in a family generally are accepted by the child. For example, substance abuse, behavioural addictions, and a culture of accepting or appreciating these disorders as the norm may be perceived by the child as non-deviant behaviours.

Compulsive buying is not a recent phenomenon as it was mentioned in the late nineteenth century by Kraepelin, the German psychiatrist who wrote about the existence of *buying maniacs* (Black 1996). There was a surge of interest in the compulsive buying phenomenon in the early 1900s during the rise of the consumer culture in the United States. Then there was another period of increased research activity starting in the 1980s when consumer behaviour researchers responded to the increased interest in the topic of consumption and consumerism (Faber and O'Guinn 2008). The problem of compulsive buyers continues to be pervasive in these modern times of consumerism.

There are many famous personalities who were said to be compulsive buyers. Black (1996) identified three cases of famous ladies whose shopping habits may be construed to be behaviours consistent with that of compulsive buyers. The first case was that of Mary Todd Lincoln (the wife of President

Lincoln), who, to the consternation of her husband and government officials, constantly overspent her budget and even was said to have used federal funds to finance her clothing shopping (Kiesel 2012). Jacqueline Kennedy Onassis was also suggested to be a victim of compulsive buying and was said to have spent $50,000 on clothes within a little over one year after President Kennedy's inauguration. The third case mentioned by Black (1996) was that of Imelda Marcos, the wife of the Philippines dictator Ferdinand Marcos, who was noted to have over 1,000 pairs of shoes, in addition to several other items of clothing, many having multiple identical copies. Unfortunately, this problem of compulsive buying is more prevalent among women shoppers (Zadka and Olajossy 2016).

THEORETICAL CONSIDERATIONS

Researchers have been trying to isolate the etiology of compulsive buying and the best consensus so far is that there is no single cause for the condition (Black 1996; Faber and O'Guinn 2008). Possible factors that are linked to compulsive buying have been grouped into classifications of psychological traits, family influence, and others (DeSarbo and Edwards 1996). Some of the psychological traits identified include dependence, denial, depression, lack of impulse control, low self-esteem, approval seeking, anxiety, escape coping tendencies, general compulsiveness, materialism, isolation, excitement seeking, and perfectionism. Factors grouped under family influence included family environment, childhood experience with money and spending, and being taught as a child to defer to others rather than think for themselves. The other group included the number of credit cards regularly used, credit debt levels, and the number of other compulsive behaviours (e.g., gambling or alcoholism) depicted by the self or parent (DeSarbo and Edwards 1996). Based on work done in recent times, researchers have been studying compulsive buying from different perspectives and utilizing different theories, a few of which are reviewed next.

Learning Theory

The learning theory provides one of the perspectives for explaining compulsive buying. This theory suggests that if a response to a situation is effective, then the response is learned and repeated, over time, by the individual. In the case of compulsive buyers, shopping would be the behaviour that was learnt and maintained since that was the response that reduced the distress caused by the need to shop (Hirschman 1992).

In utilizing the framework of learning theory to explain the compulsive buying behaviour, Hirschman (1992) described two types of personalities related to compulsive buying addicts—the distressed and the sociopathic types. The distressed personality is constantly enshrouded with feelings of low esteem and self-doubt and other personality issues which may cause symptoms like depression. To control or manage the emotional turmoil, the individual with this personality typically turns to an external behaviour to reduce the emotional condition, which helps to remove the focus from the condition. If the behaviour, like shopping, seems to be successful in relieving the distress, then this reinforces itself and the person repeatedly turns to the same behaviour in times of distress. Initially, the person may even set boundaries on how much and how often this self-medicating occurs. But soon these boundaries may be breached as the person repeatedly returns to the behaviour until a point is reached where the person finds that it becomes difficult and then impossible to refrain from the behaviour. For the sociopathic personality type, these individuals are more involved in pursuing the pleasure reward of the activity in which they indulge and reflect less guilt in the repercussions of the behaviour. Such a person, upon experiencing significant pleasure in the process of shopping, may repeatedly return to this behaviour just to enjoy the pleasure of immediate gratification. Repeated reinforcement of this behaviour results in the individual finding it difficult and even impossible to control it.

Social Cognitive Theory

The Social Cognitive Theory provides a self-regulatory approach for dealing with compulsive buying. LaRose (2001) suggested that the classical learning theory is inadequate as a framework for compulsive buying, as it lacks the ability to explain the self-control aspect of human behaviour. LaRose (2001) also noted that since the lack of self-control is a core feature of unregulated buying, the Social Cognitive Theory, which provides an explanation of regulating behaviour would be better suited to explain compulsive buying. According to the Social Cognitive Theory, which was formulated by Bandura (1989), people can regulate their behaviour by observing consequences to actions in the external environment and processing this information for adjusting their behaviour. Basically, proponents of the Social Cognitive Theory believe that the internal personal factors, the external environment and the behaviour all operate on each other. Thus, for example, the internal and external factors directly influence behaviour. In turn, the internal factors and behaviour also influence the external factors. Similarly, the external factors and behaviour affect the internal factors. These all operate in turn, with any two of the three factors influencing the third factor, with the strength of the influence from each not necessarily the same as the others at any given time. Using the framework of social cognitive *theory*, the individual falls into the addiction of compulsive buying (behaviour) when the self-regulatory factor of self-observation is disrupted by uncontrollable urges (internal), triggered by the shopping stimuli (external).

Theory of the Leisure Class (Conspicuous Consumption)

The theory of conspicuous consumption, outlined initially by Veblen in 1918, has been used as a framework to understand compulsive consumption. This theory suggests that people engage in conspicuous consumption primarily as a means to bolster their self-image. Shoppers who engage in conspicuous consumption are often affected by low esteem (Thornquist 2017). Further, several researchers have found that self-esteem is one of the antecedents of compulsive buying (Yurchisin and Johnson 2004). In using the theory of conspicuous consumption as a framework, Thornquist (2017) posited that compulsive buying is really a reflection of the need to repair the self-image because of the low-esteem issue, and that compulsive buyers tend to be more fashion conscious and interested in how they are seen and perceived by others, thus engaging in conspicuous consumption.

Jacob's General Theory of Addiction

Jacob's General Theory of Addiction explains the addictive dimension of compulsive buying. The theory explains that people engage in addictive behaviours such as gambling or alcoholism as a form of self-treatment that permits an escape from their stress-like conditions with the belief that this addictive behaviour will momentarily alleviate their stressful situation (Gupta and Derevensky 1998). Addictive behaviours are associated with immediate gratification that can either be physical or psychological and this gratification is believed to perpetuate the addiction (Jacobs 1989).

MOOD MANAGEMENT

Mood management is another perspective that provides a part of the explanation for compulsive buying. People may rely on shopping as a means to alleviate negative moods or to create, heighten, or extend positive moods (Faber and O'Guinn 2008). Interviews of known compulsive shoppers have elicited views that their moods immediately improved after shopping (Faber and O'Guinn 2008), and many compulsive shoppers do not want nor actually use the items purchased. In an attempt to alter their moods, people have relied on shopping to do so, and the repetitive buying behaviour can lead to the point of addiction (Elliott 1994).

Escape Theory

Escape theory has been used by researchers to explain binge eating (Paxton and Diggens 1996) and suicide (Baumeister 1990). This theory suggests that there is a "tendency for people to engage in behaviours to avoid an unpleasant psychological reaction. Escape theory is used to describe behaviours that enable a person to flee from negative perceptions of the self" (Baumeister and Vohs 2007a, 313). With narrowing, the person seeks to shift attention from the negative perception of self to an activity like shopping that detracts from the self-image. In doing so, the person narrows focus to the shopping activity which allows the person to escape the thoughts of the self-image that is causing the distress. The irony is that repetitive indulgence in the escape activity, like shopping, in the end causes its own distress when it becomes addictive.

Baumeister and Vohs (2007a) identified six steps in the escape theory.

1. The person encounters a severe experience which brings him/her to the realization that current circumstances fall below societal or self-imposed standards.
2. The person blames these disappointing circumstances on aspects of his/her personality as opposed to situational factors.
3. The person recognizes that the current circumstances portrays him/herself as inadequate, incompetent, unattractive, or guilty.
4. The person experiences negative emotions when confronting the realisation that the current circumstances fall below desired expectations.
5. The person seeks to escape from this negative psychological reaction by seeking to avoid thinking about the circumstances.
6. The lack of restraint in avoiding the negative thoughts may lead to undesirable behaviours.

Each of the steps depends on the preceding step, therefore for a person to indulge in an undesirable behaviour, he or she must have worked through each of the previous five steps (Baumeister and Vohs 2007a).

THEORETICAL CONSIDERATIONS SUMMARIZED

Each of these theoretical considerations provides a frame for addressing the phenomenon of compulsive buying. The learning theory explains that compulsive buying is developed when the shopping activity is learnt and then repeated over time, because shopping proved to be effective in relieving stress. The Social Cognitive Theory provides a self-regulatory framework—since proponents of this approach believe that compulsive buying is a breakdown in the self-control mechanism. In the case of the conspicuous consumption theory, this theory suggests that people engage in conspicuous consumption primarily as a means to bolster their self-image because of a low-esteem condition. Jacob's general theory of addiction outlines that people engage in addictive behaviours such as gambling, alcoholism, or compulsive buying as a form of self-treatment that permits an escape from their stress-like conditions. The mood management perspective indicates that people may rely on shopping as a means to alleviate negative moods or to create, heighten, or extend positive moods. Engaging in this activity repetitively gives rise to compulsive buying. The escape theory suggests that people engage in behaviours in order to escape negative perceptions of self. Repetitive engagement in the escape activity such as shopping may lead to compulsive buying. Other theories that are relevant to explaining or mitigating compulsive buying include the self-regulation theory (Baumeister and Vohs 2007b) and regulatory focus theory (Higgins 1998). These other theories will be discussed in detail in chapter 5 in relation to their applications for self-regulating compulsive buying behaviour.

CLASSIFICATION OF COMPULSIVE BUYING BEHAVIOUR

There is no agreement among compulsive buying behaviour researchers about a common definition of the disorder, or even where to classify it among the plethora of other mental disorders. As noted by Harnish, Bridges, and Karelitz (2017), although this disorder is very serious and is also a growing phenomenon, it was not mentioned in the latest (fifth) edition of *The American Psychiatric Association's Diagnostic and Statistical Manual of Mental Disorders* (DSM-5)—the main document relied on by professionals for psychiatric diagnoses. Harnish, Bridges, and Karelitz (2017) further contended that the disorder did not make the list for the World Health Organization's (WHO) international classification of diseases. This is in spite of the fact that many of the definitions of the behaviour concur that it is a psychiatric condition, that it is quite widespread, occurring in several countries (Benson and Eisenach 2013), that it has several serious repercussions in several areas of the lives of those affected by the disorder (Granero et al. 2016), and that it is a growing phenomenon (Dittmar 2005). Even though compulsive buying was not included in DSM-5, two other behavioural disorders, gambling disorder and internet gaming disorder, were incorporated in the manual (Pinna et al. 2015).

The fact that compulsive buying behaviour is excluded from the DSM-5 and the WHO international classification is surprising, since the condition has been researched for over one hundred years, and has also increased in prevalence in recent years (Granero et al. 2016). Granero et al. (2016) also noted that the gambling disorder shares several important features with compulsive buying. One of the important features is that both disorders have impulsive/compulsive characteristics, and so it is surprising that gambling disorder was included in DSM-5 and compulsive buying behaviour was not. It may, therefore, be the right time to call for more official recognition of compulsive buying behaviour as a public health problem so that more resources can be made available for more research, identification, and treatment, and, if possible, prevention. A first step could be for compulsive buying behaviour to be classified as a mental health disorder in the next edition of the DSM. Despite not being classified, there is increasing research in the area—from both the psychiatric and psychological perspectives (Chinomona 2013).

For contextual purposes, it is worth noting that compulsive buying is one of a long list of behavioural addictions which includes sex addiction, exercise addiction, workaholism, and as mentioned before, gambling and internet gaming. Most of these addictions were omitted from being included in DSM-5 because of "insufficient evidence, poor description of the clinical course of the behaviour and the need to establish diagnostic criteria in order to classify these behaviours as mental disorders" (Pinna et al. 2015, 380).

Despite the omission of compulsive buying in the DSM-5, Goldsmith and McElroy (2000) proposed diagnostic criteria and treatment for compulsive buying, and other researchers have noted positive results using anti-depressants such as naltrexone, bupropion, fluoxetine, and nortriptyline (Grant 2003; Benson and Gengler 2004; Faber and Christenson 1996). The mental health professionals have successfully diagnosed the disorder (Dittmar 2004) and have also utilized non-drug therapeutic methods to treat it (Benson and Gengler 2004).

Compulsive buying has been researched for a long time, however to date, there has not been a consensus on how to classify this behaviour, as it may be related to addictive disorders (Coombs 2004), obsessive-compulsive disorders (Nichols 2018), impulse control disorders (Koran et al. 2002), or mood disorders (Gregory 2020). The marketing literature also suggests that compulsive buying may be classified as a stimulus response shopping problem.

It is not clear which of these classifications that compulsive buying is related to. A brief discussion on the possible classification for locating compulsive buying follows.

Addictive Disorder

There are three primary factors that can be used to identify an addiction—diminished control, craving and tolerance (Fauth-Bühler, Mann, and Potenza 2016). Diminished control is the evidence that the person has a reduction in the ability to limit or terminate the substance abuse or behaviour that is addictive and harmful. Typically, the victim tries, several times, to either reduce or stop the use of the addictive substance or the behaviour but usually fails. The negative implications of the addictive behaviour do not usually provide enough of an incentive for the individual to regain control.

Craving is the overwhelming and uncontrollable urge to consume the addictive substance or indulge in the addictive behaviour. The individual has to satisfy the craving despite the obvious negative consequences. When this craving is satisfied repeatedly, this creates tolerance. Tolerance is the need to constantly increase the amount and frequency of the dosage of the substance, or instance of the behaviour to achieve the same feeling of euphoria and/or temporary diminished craving.

Hagedorn and Hartwig Moorhead (2010, 68) outlined how a former client described the addictive experience:

> An insidious characteristic of addictive disorders is the drive for the "perfect high," aptly described . . . as "a speeding train, rolling down the tracks, rolling right through me, making me feel perfectly strong, perfectly beautiful, and perfectly invincible." Unfortunately, each time that they tried to catch the "train" (i.e., the strength and power of their initial experiences), the locomotive moved farther away and quickly careened out of control.

Coombs (2004) explained that all disorders can be characterized by compulsive actions or behaviour, loss of control, and continued use despite adverse consequences. In addition, it has been found that at the initial stages of these disorders, the person displaying these symptoms is initially motivated by certain types of rewards that cause them to persist with the behaviour.

Obsessive-Compulsive Disorder

Obsessive-compulsive disorder (OCD) is a mental health condition which involves intrusive obsessions and repetitive compulsions (Williams et al.

2013). The obsessive aspect of this disorder includes unwanted thoughts or impulses that increase anxiety. The compulsive aspect involves repetitive actions that are employed in decreasing anxiety. There are several types of obsessive-compulsive disorder. This chapter provides a summary of five of the more common types.

Checking—People with the OCD checking type disorder have the excessive urge to repetitively check and confirm any of a range of disparate things (Williams et al. 2013). Examples include checking if the doors were locked or checking if the stove was turned off. This checking may take place even hundreds of times within a fairly short timeframe and felt to be mandatory in the mind of the sufferer—even to the detriment of any other important appointments, commitments or required tasks. This can be very distressing to the sufferer as the impulse to check repetitively is perceived to be uncontrollable. Checking behaviour makes up the majority of compulsive acts performed by people with OCD.

Contamination—A person afflicted with the OCD condition of contamination is always excessively preoccupied with preventing any contact with germs (Williams et al. 2013). Symptoms of this disorder include not wanting to shake the hands of other people, fear of being in crowds, and being afraid of touching anything in public such as stair rails or door knobs. This uncontrollable fear of contamination may also propel the person to be constantly cleaning the house—especially kitchens and bathrooms.

Hoarding—Hoarding is the accumulation of items without discarding or parting with these items even when they have little or no value (Williams et al. 2013). A key feature of hoarding is that the person finds it difficult to discard the items because they believe that they will need them in the future.

Unwanted Thoughts—Unwanted thoughts are involuntary and frequent thoughts that are difficult to be removed from the person's mind (Williams et al. 2013). Symptoms of this type of OCD includes invasive thoughts which typically urge the sufferer to commit violent and other horrific acts. The thoughts may be suicidal in nature or involve killing someone else, so the person with these symptoms experiences severe distress and suffers because of an inability to stop these thoughts.

Symmetry and Ordering—People with the OCD type symmetry and ordering tend to be perfectionists and have the uncontrollable preoccupation with keeping items neat and organized (Williams et al. 2013). They may experience discomfort if items in their environment such as books and plates are not in a straight line or in a neat and orderly manner. People with this type of OCD reduce their discomfort and distress when they organize the items.

Impulse Control Disorders

Impulse control disorders (ICDs) involve the inability of persons to control impulses in social and occupational circumstances, and which sometimes lead to personal, social, and even legal problems (Grant, Odlaug, and Kim 2013). Grant, Odlaug, and Kim (2013) noted that the full extent of ICDs is not understood, however they do share the following features:

- Repetitive engagement in a particular behaviour even if there are adverse results;
- Reduced control over the problem behaviour; and
- Prior to engaging in the behaviour, there is a surge in craving for the behaviour.

Mood Disorders

A mood disorder manifests itself as a disturbance in a person's mood for a prolonged period, and the mood has no apparent situational cause (DuRubeis et al. 2016). Typically, one experiences a range of emotions based on various achievements, activities, or situations in one's life. For example, one may be exultant after finally landing a new job, or sad and despondent after losing a loved one. However, when a person has mood disorder, the moods control the person's life and disrupts relationships. The mood changes generally occur without being triggered by any external circumstances. According to DuRubeis et al. (2016) there are two main classes of mood disorders, depressive and bipolar.

Depressive Disorder

Symptoms of depressive disorder include loss of appetite, loss of interest in pleasurable activities, pervasive negative feelings, and general feelings of apathy (DuRubeis et al. 2016). The person suffering from this disorder may also have suicidal thoughts and bouts of insomnia. An episode of depressive disorder could last for two weeks or more.

Bipolar Disorder

A person with bipolar disorder constantly has mood swings that are not triggered by any apparent circumstances (Parekh 2017). People displaying symptoms of bipolar disorder usually have mood swings from one extreme of mania (called a manic episode) to another extreme of depression (called a depressive episode). During the manic episode, which can last for one or more weeks, the person with the disorder has more energy than normal and can either be in very high spirits or irritable during the period. At other times the person experiences severe cases of depression and apathy, sometimes accompanied by feelings of hopelessness, and this may last for two weeks or more. At other times, when not displaying either extreme moods, the person will appear to be normal.

STIMULUS-RESPONSE SHOPPING PROBLEM

Compulsive buying is also classified as a stimulus-response shopping problem as it resembles impulsive buying. The shopping stimuli are provided through store front displays and advertisements, and the compulsive buyer responds by making the purchase. This phenomenon is popularly discussed in the marketing literature on consumer behaviour. Compulsive consumption represents a large portion of consumer sales hence the phenomenon is of interest to the firm. Marketers, therefore, have both a financial opportunity and an ethical responsibility in the service they provide to this vulnerable group. These ethical considerations will be further discussed in chapter 6.

ISSUES RELATED TO COMPULSIVE BUYING

There are some important issues related to compulsive buying such as the *guilt and remorse* that typically follows after a compulsive buying episode, and the *pain of paying*. These and other issues are briefly reviewed next.

Buyer's High

Buyer's high is the intense excitement that the compulsive buyer experiences while shopping (Heshmat 2018). This may be compared to the chemically induced high experienced by substance abusers. The pleasurable feeling of getting high becomes addictive for the compulsive shopper, and subsequently the person reaches the point where the urge to repeat this high becomes irresistible. From the perspective of the compulsive buyer, the activity of shopping is separate from the actual item that is purchased because the buying is what brings the fleeting high. It does not matter what is being purchased as many of the purchased items remain unopened, some of these items are given to family and friends (Workman and Paper 2010) and some of the items are just hoarded (Hayward and Coles 2009).

Shopping to Dampen Unpleasant Emotions

Compulsive buying is also done to repress depression, anxiety or other unpleasant emotions, and the shopping is viewed as the antidote for the unpleasant emotions (Heshmat 2018). However, since the dampening of the unpleasant emotions is only temporary, the shopping activity has to be repeated whenever the unpleasant emotions return.

Guilt and Remorse

Feelings of guilt and remorse are associated with compulsive buyers (Heshmat 2018). After the negative emotions are assuaged with shopping, the compulsive shopper, typically, then has to confront the fact that the purchases are not needed, and sometimes cannot be afforded. This subsequently triggers guilt and remorse. The person displaying the disorder is disappointed because after the shopping there is the distress when the lack of self-control is acknowledged. There are also the issues relating to the financial crises that result from uncontrollable spending (Kuzma and Black 2006).

THE PAIN OF PAYING

There is some amount of mental pain or anguish when a person parts with money (Ariely and Kreisler 2017). MRI scans show that the displeasure of paying, which increases when making higher payments, stimulates the same areas of the brain that are stimulated when there is physical pain (Ariely and Kreiser 2017). The results from experiments regarding the duration of time between the actual payment and the consumption of items purchased revealed that "because of the pain of paying, we are willing to pay more before, less after, and even less during consumption of the very same product" (Ariely and Kreiser 2017, 74). Furthermore, if less attention is paid to the act of making a payment, then this would also reduce the pain of paying. The credit card is a facility that increases the time between payment and consumption and allows one to pay less attention to the actual paying process. Being able to swipe takes away the attention that one would normally pay to taking out the cash, handling it, counting it, and turning it over to someone else. The credit card also creates a time lag between the payment and the consumption of the purchased items. These two features of the credit card, therefore, decrease the pain of paying and make it easier to complete a purchase, thus facilitating compulsive buying. According to Ariely and Kreiser (2017, 81), "not only are people more willing to pay when they use credit cards, but also that they make larger purchases, leave larger tips, are more likely to underestimate or forget how much they spent, and make spending decisions more quickly."

Much more money is, therefore, spent with the use of credit cards than would normally be spent using cash (Soll, Keeney, and Larrick 2013). It is also much easier to accumulate debt faster as spending, even when done recently, is more easily forgotten when credit cards are used. The use of credit cards is a major factor in the phenomenon of compulsive buying and a review of its history, function, consequences of its use, and abuse by marketers are further discussed in chapter 4.

CLOSING COMMENTS

This chapter reviewed some of the theoretical considerations and possible disorders that compulsive buying may be related to. Compulsive buying may be associated with addictive disorders, obsessive-compulsive disorders, impulse control disorders, mood disorders, and stimulus-response shopping problems. In a study reported by Lejoyeux and Weinstein (2010), they discovered that patients who had compulsive buying behaviours were also found to have addictive disorders, mood disorders, or obsessive-compulsive disorders. This illustrates the problem of classification of compulsive buying as it is not clear where it is located among these disorders. This unsettled problem of classification of compulsive buying may have contributed to the exclusion of this disorder from the latest DSM-5. More research is required for locating compulsive buying among addictive disorders as this is seen as a serious and growing phenomenon (Harnish, Bridges, and Karelitz 2017). The chapter also discussed other topical issues pertaining to compulsive buying. These include the guilt and remorse that is associated with the problem, and the pain of paying, which can be increased with the use of cash or decreased with the use of the credit card.

Chapter Two

Personality, Personality Traits, and Consumer Traits

INTRODUCTION

This chapter addresses the context for relating personality traits to compulsive buying making reference to the equivalence between basic personality traits and consumer traits. Consumer traits are characteristics of individual differences that represent consistent patterns of thoughts, feelings, and behaviours that are applied to the consumer (Joachimsthaler and Lastovicka 1984).

These traits are mere subsets of the more basic personality traits which are individual difference characteristics applied across a wide range of human domains, situations and context (Steenkamp and Maydeu-Olivares 2015). Indeed, many scholars have agreed that consumer traits are entrenched in basic personality traits (Joachimsthaler and Lastovicka 1984; Lastovicka 1982; Raju 1980) and consist of psychological characteristics, social group influences, demographic characteristics, and consumer state-of-mind characteristics (Johnson and Rhee 2008).

These consumer traits are very complex but can be studied and better understood through personality trait theories of which there are two influential schools of thought. The first school believes that all individuals have the same set of personality traits and individual differences are explained by the degree to which these traits are displayed in one individual versus another. The second school believes that individual differences are explained through trait combinations. Everyone has a specific set of personality traits, but not all traits. In addition, everyone has a unique combination of traits making one individual characteristically different from another.

This chapter traces the early research on basic personality traits and highlights the seminal work of Allport and Odbert (1936) which provides an exhaustive list of four thousand personality trait-type predispositions. The role of the Big 5 Personality Traits (openness, conscientiousness, extraversion, agreeableness, and neuroticism) in explaining individual differences was also highlighted. Notably, the big five personality traits, which are typically classified as basic traits, are treated as consumer traits in studies such as Steenkamp and Maydeu-Olivares (2015) and Otero-López and Villardefrancos (2013) thus highlighting a blurred line between basic and consumer traits. Unlike basic personality traits, there are no generally accepted classifications of consumer traits and the latter traits are only different in their sole application to consumption (Steenkamp and Maydeu-Olivares 2015).

The works of Mowen and Spears (1999) and Mowen (2000) that gave rise to the 3M Theory were also explored in this chapter. This theory is utilized for explaining consumer behavioural outcomes from a set of personality-type predictors. In highlighting the role of consumer traits in compulsive buying, the chapter draws on the prior research and provides scenarios and examples for explicating this role.

There are many consumer predispositions that could influence the phenomenon of compulsive buying. These predispositions are internal to the consumer and include attitudes, moods, motivation and consumer traits. Similarly, there are external conditions (e.g., family, society and culture) and situational context (e.g., loss of job or death of loved ones) that could influence this behaviour. Compulsive buying is, therefore, a very complex behaviour as it could be triggered by so many predispositions, conditions, and situations which themselves could operate either singly or in combination, thus making the triggers of compulsive behaviour very confounding and rendering any scientific explanation of this behaviour to be a work-in-progress at best. However, there is consensus in research which suggests that consumer traits provide at least a part of the explanation for buying behavioural outcomes such as brand loyalty (Smith 2015), gambling activities (Fang and Mowen 2009), credit card misuse (Pirog and Roberts 2007), and negative consumption-based emotions (Mooradian and Olver 1997).

This trait approach was found to be a best fit for addressing the buyer behavioural problem of compulsive buying for several reasons. First, individual differences, which characterize consumer traits, account for a significant portion of the variability in consumer consumption (Mowen 2000). This means that the consumer personality explains a large portion of the reasons as to how and why we consume. Second, many consumer predispositions, including compulsive buying, are trait-like in nature and can, therefore, be modelled using trait theories for a good fit. For example, to have a vanity predisposition or an attitude to status consumption are trait-like constructs which could be modelled using the Meta-theoretic Model of Motivation and Personality (3M Theory) for predicting compulsive buying from these constructs.

This chapter, therefore, focused on the pivotal role that consumer traits play in compulsive buying behaviour and sets the stage for the development of an empirical model (chapter 3) for validating this role.

PERSONALITY PSYCHOLOGY

The name Sigmund Freud is one of and probably the most well-known names in the realm of psychology, in general, and definitely in the domain of personality psychology, more specifically. Most of what is known today about personality psychology is attributed either directly to Freud's research, or based on research that is built on Freud's work, or based on studies that have disputed Freud's work (Schultz and Schultz 2017).

There are several branches or domains in the realm of psychology (and the number keeps growing)—with different sources providing totally different numbers depending on the method of classification. For example, Cherry (2017) listed twenty-six branches, while Brazier (2018) only reported nine branches. Whatever the number of branches, however, personality psychology is listed in the literature as one of the main branches, and significant work was done in this area by Sigmund Freud to make this branch popular. In his work on personality psychology, Freud utilized psychoanalysis as the primary method for undertaking his case studies.

According to Kunst (2014), psychoanalysis is the psychotherapy provided by a trained psychologist or psychiatrist, using frequent meetings with the patient in an attempt to resolve psychological issues. The goal of these sessions is to uncover the root of the problem which may have been caused by some childhood experiences, or other situations in one's past, which are thought to be hidden in the patient's subconscious.

As indicated before, Freud's primary research method was the use of several sessions of psychoanalysis with his patients. From his research, Freud posited that a person is primarily driven by instincts, the driving forces of the personality that determine behaviour. Furthermore, Freud thought that there were three levels of personality—the conscious, preconscious, and unconscious. He later revised this structure and replaced it with the idea that the human personality consists of three interactive systems, namely, the id, the super ego, and the ego (Schultz and Schultz 2017).

The id, thought to be the primary component of the personality typology, serves as the "reservoir for the instincts and the libido" (Schultz and Schultz 2017, 45) and provides an impulsive driving force for satisfying basic urges, needs and desires. Schiffman and Kanuk (2009) explained that the superego is akin to a moral compass and represents the individual's internal expression of societal and ethical norms. The authors also indicated that the ego, or the third component of the personality typology, provides a balancing act between the id and the superego and serves to consciously balance the impulsive demands of the id against the societal and ethical constraints of the superego.

The conflicts that take place among the three components of the personality system during one's childhood development are instrumental in producing the unique personality that is formulated within each individual. In addition, the unique relationships and situations that an individual experiences during the early developmental stages also contribute to the casting of the personality.

Whereas Freud's perspective of personality was psychoanalytical, Jung, who was initially a disciple of Freud, formulated what he later described as analytical personality (Schultz and Schultz 2017). Jung's perspective of personality was that it consisted of many aspects that interact with each other. Also, whereas Freud believed that the past was the primary shaper of an individual's personality, Jung believed that in addition to the past, the personality is also shaped by aspirations of the future.

Jung's personality structure consisted of the ego (the part of the personality related to consciousness) and opposing attitudes of extraversion and introversion. The conflict between the opposing attitudes and the ego are the drivers of personality formation, and hence determine the behaviour of the individual. The result of this constant conflict and interaction formulates different personality types, and Jung proposed eight such types—Extraverted thinking, Extraverted feeling, Extraverted sensing, Extraverted intuiting, Introverted thinking, Introverted feeling, Introverted sensing, and Introverted intuiting.

Many readers would immediately recognize these personality types with the very popular personality assessment instrument known as the Myers-Briggs, which was developed based on Jung's personality types.

The contribution of Adler to the domain of personality psychology is also important to mention as we continue this high level review of the evolution of research in this important area. Adler rejected the views by Freud that personality was developed by biological instincts over which the individual had little to no control. He believed that personality was formed based on the social and situational interactions and relationships unique to the individual, who is consciously involved in the creation of his or her unique personality (Schultz and Schultz 2017). A significant contribution to the domain of personality psychology is Adler's perspective of the important role of birth order in the formation of one's personality.

Adler's views were that even though children were born in the same family and circumstances, each child actually experienced markedly different social situations, some of which can be attributed to birth order. In this perspective, the firstborn child usually is the object of much affection by the new parents. The impact on the first child, of the birth of the second child, depends primarily on the length of time between the birth of the first and the second, and also on how much pampering was received by the first prior to the birth of the second child. The more pampering and the shorter the time between births would have a greater impact on the first child, who would experience a "sense of dethronement" (Schultz and Schultz 2017, 118) upon the birth of the second child. Based on this, the personality of the first born was thought to be "often oriented toward the past, locked in nostalgia, and pessimistic about the future" (p. 117).

According to Adler's model, "the second child always has the example of the older child's behaviour as a model, a threat, or a source of competition" (Schultz and Schultz 2017, 119) and so the personality of the second child is typically "more optimistic about the future and are likely to be competitive and ambitious" (p. 119).

The youngest child, according to the model derived by Adler, may become high or over achievers based on the desire to surpass the older siblings. On the other hand, if the parents pampered the youngest too much, he or she may over rely on others, and not learn the need to strive, thus becoming helpless and have a hard time adjusting to adulthood.

If there is only one child in the family, he or she may have difficulty adjusting to the outside world with the sudden realisation of no longer being the only centre of attraction, as it was within the family circle. Although this perspective by Adler has become fairly pervasive, an extensive study by Rohrer, Egloff and Schmukle (2015), using a research sample of over twenty thousand persons from Germany, Great Britain, and the United States, seem to disprove Adler's views. Even though this study by Rofrer, Egloff, and Schmukle found that intelligence declined from the first born to the other siblings, it also importantly found no relationship between birth order and personality.

Our brief discussion on personality psychology has so far highlighted some of the seminal work in this area. The early researchers thought that personality of the individual was the antecedent to the behaviour and this has continued to be the line of thinking. We noted that Freud started by explaining that personality was primarily driven by instincts while subsequent researchers (Adler and Jung) thought that personality was not only driven by the internal state, but also by external triggers.

PERSONALITY AND PERSONALITY TRAITS

Personality relates to all the characteristics, qualities and features of a person that make that person unique and different from all other persons. Personality is like a fingerprint and is the sum total of all the physical, mental, social, and emotional aspects of a person (Schultz and Schultz 2017). It may seem that personality is shaped by several factors, including internal genetic components and also by environmental factors. However, "heredity provides the personality with raw materials, such as physique, intelligence, and temperament that may then be shaped, expanded, or limited by the conditions of our environment" (p. 197).

Unlike a person's fingerprint, a person's personality is much harder to identify, define, and capture. If, indeed, the personality could be easily captured like the fingerprint, it may prove to be able to uniquely identify an individual. However, it may take a lifetime to study an individual's personality—and even then the nebulous borders of that personality may never be capable of being plotted, or the depths of it fathomed.

Allport (1968) also confronted the possibility that the sum total of the personality contained within an individual may very well be unknowable—but thought that with the proper perspective and appropriate measuring tools, progress may be made by studying slices of the personality at a time, or the traits or personal dispositions. Allport, known to be one of the pioneers of the trait perspective of personality, outlined some assertions he had previously made, and subsequently revised, about these traits. He noted that a trait, (Allport 1968, 44):

1. has more than nominal existence;
2. is more generalized than a habit;
3. is dynamic, or at least determinative, in behaviour;
4. may be established empirically;
5. is only relatively independent of other traits;
6. is not synonymous with moral or social judgement;
7. may be viewed either in the light of the personality which contains it, or in the light of its distribution in the population at large; and
8. that [is] inconsistent with [another] trait [is] not proof of the nonexistence of the trait.

Allport (1968) concluded that for a better understanding of the personality of the individual, the researcher should pursue a study of the trait characteristics.

SEMINAL WORK ON PERSONALITY TRAITS

Research on personality traits and the factors used to represent taxonomies of these traits have been pursued since the 1900s (John, Angleitner, and Ostendorf,

1988). In the early days of such research, there was pervasive chaos, first because many of the researchers were English, German, and Dutch, and so a fundamental issue that existed at the time was the simple definition of the terms used by the various researchers. Such a nomenclature for the field of personality traits was quite varied and nebulous. However, the seminal work by Allport and Odbert (1936) provided an exhaustive listing of four thousand traits extracted from the 1925 version of *Webster's New International Dictionary*. The list was arranged alphabetically under four columns—Personal Traits, Temporary States, Social Evaluations, and Metaphorical and Doubtful. Allport and Odbert justified the usefulness and importance of their laborious effort in naming the personality traits by noting that "more than a century ago Jeremy Bentham maintained that the chief obstacle to clear thinking lay in the confused process of naming" (p. 1).

Cattell and Nesselroade (1967) approached personality psychology from a different perspective from the psychoanalytic approach used by Freud. Instead of the goal of changing abnormal personality to normal—which was Freud's approach—the goal was to predict behaviour given the situational context (Schultz and Schultz 2017). Cattell and Nesselroade (1967) demonstrated that there were sixteen unique personality traits (Schultz and Schultz 2017; Bourke, Francis, and Robbins 2004). This was of significance because an important area in personality research was the number of factors in which the numerous observed personality behaviours could be clustered. Several instruments were also developed to measure personality traits, of which the most popular is called the Sixteen Personality Factor (16 PF) questionnaire. A list of Cattell's sixteen factors is given below (Ellis, Abrams, and Abrams 2009).

1. Warmth (warm vs. reserved)
2. Reasoning (less vs. more intelligent)
3. Emotional stability (low vs. high ego strength)
4. Dominance (dominant vs. submissive)
5. Liveliness (serious vs. spontaneous)
6. Rule-consciousness
7. Social boldness
8. Sensitivity
9. Vigilance (trusting vs. suspicious)
10. Abstractedness (practical vs. imaginative)
11. Privateness (open vs. shrewd)
12. Apprehension (fearful vs. self-assured)
13. Openness to change
14. Self-reliance
15. Perfectionism (neat and careful vs. disordered)
16. Tension (nervous vs. relaxed)

Eysenck (1951) also introduced a personality typology consisting of three factors—extraversion, neuroticism, and psychoticism and other traits within a hierarchical model. These three factors identified are at the highest level of abstraction in this model.

The Big Five or Five Factor Model

Researchers believed that the disparity between the number of traits proposed by Eysenck and Cattell (three versus sixteen) were either too few or too many and so research continued on the subject. Among the researchers were Mc-Crae and Costa (2004) who, after extensive research, derived five factors of personality which are still thought to be the most robust of the personality typologies (Schultz and Schultz 2017).

The Big Five or Five Factor Model consists of five factors—Neuroticism, Extraversion, Openness to Experience, Agreeableness, and Conscientious-ness. A brief discussion follows.

Neuroticism—People who are highly neurotic are typically psychologi-cally unstable and display negative emotions such as anxiety, sadness, ner-vousness, and pessimism (Woo and Ahn 2015; Quintelier 2014; McCrae and Costa 1999), and are "abnormally sensitive" (Shehzadi et al. 2016, 417). Schultz and Schultz (2017) noted that "neuroticism has been negatively re-lated to emotional well-being" (p. 234). In terms of the effects of neuroticism on behaviour, Barelds (2005) found that couples had better marriages when both partners were low on neuroticism. Similarly, Andreassen et al. (2013) found that "Neuroticism was positively associated with Internet addiction, exercise addiction, compulsive buying, and study addiction" (p. 90), and research by Shehzadi et al. (2016) indicated compulsive buying and neuroti-cism have a direct positive relationship.

Extraversion—People who are extraverts are typically outgoing and so-ciable, have many friends, and love to participate in events, functions, and activities which involve other people (Woo and Ahn 2015; Quintelier 2014; McCrae and Costa 1999). According to Schultz and Schultz (2017), studies undertaken in three different countries showed that "extraversion was related to happiness, optimism, and life satisfaction" (p. 234). As such extroverts can be easily identified wherever you go, and similarly those who lie somewhere at the other end of the spectrum, introverts, can also be easily identified. Extraverts are more externally focused, gravitate to other people, known or unknown, and are the fun of the party. They laugh more, talk more, are more affectionate, and are generally more fun to be around. On the other hand, per-sons low on the extraversion scale, the introverts, prefer to be by themselves and avoid excitement and places where many people gather (Schultz and

Schultz 2017). Barelds (2005) also found that extraversions in both individuals in a marriage contributed to better marital relationships. Also, Andreassen et al. (2013) found that "Extraversion was positively associated with Facebook addiction, exercise addiction, mobile phone addiction, and compulsive buying" (p. 90).

Openness to Experience—People who are open to experience, typically, are flexible minded, curious, and adaptable. They are high on the openness scale and would be open to new experiences, new products, new hobbies, new tastes, and new ideas. These persons' perspectives would be confined not just to the space and environment around them but would be outward looking—loving to travel and explore new places and things (Woo and Ahn 2015; Quintelier 2014; McCrae and Costa 1999). People who are high in openness tend to be more intelligent and have many intellectual interests (Schultz and Shultz 2017). Andreassen et al. (2013) also found that "Openness to Experience was negatively associated with Facebook addiction and mobile phone addiction" (p. 90), and research by Paunonen (2003) indicated that compulsive buyers score low on openness to new experiences.

Agreeableness—Words used to describe people who are high on agreeableness are forgiving, trusting, easy-going, cooperative, selfless, altruistic, and modest (Woo and Ahn 2015; Quintelier 2014; McCrae and Costa 1999; Schultz and Shultz 2017). Agreeable persons, typically, have and maintain good relations with others, and display selfless traits, even to the point of being thought of as push overs. Andreassen et al. (2013) found that "Agreeableness was negatively associated with Internet addiction, exercise addiction, mobile phone addiction, and compulsive buying" (p. 90). In their twenty-five year prospective study, Laursen, Pulkkinen, and Adams (2002) noted the strong impact of the personality trait of agreeableness, and indicated that it is "one of the most salient and influential personality construct" (p. 591), which had the feature whereby it "appears to enhance the benefits of positive traits, and its absence appears to exacerbate the detrimental impact of less desirable traits" (p. 600). One of their important findings pertaining to agreeableness was that "Adults with the advantageous combination of high agreeableness, high socialization, and low impulsivity reported less alcoholism and depression, fewer arrests, and more career stability than did those with the unfavourable combination of low agreeableness, low socialization, and high impulsivity" (p. 600).

Conscientiousness—People who are conscientious are typically very organized, try to comply with rules and social norms, and usually think before acting. This last characteristic usually translates into the conscientious person being more given to doing long-term planning and possessing other leadership skills (Woo and Ahn 2015; Quintelier 2014; McCrae and Costa 1999).

Andreassen et al. (2013) found that "conscientiousness was negatively associated with Facebook addiction, video game addiction, Internet addiction, and compulsive buying and positively associated with exercise addiction and study addiction" (p. 90).

A Note on the Big Five

Digman (1990), in a review of the literature on the factoring of personality traits, hailed the emergence of the Five Factor Model and commented that "the Big Five have appeared now in at least five languages, leading one to suspect that something quite fundamental is involved here" (p. 433). However, as Digman noted, while there seemed to be significant agreement among researchers regarding the number of personality factors, this is not the case regarding the naming of these five factors, nor the meaning of the terms.

The HEXACO Model

Ashton and Lee (2009) opined that even though there are several instruments that reliably measure the big five factors, the origin of these five factors were based on lexical analysis confined to the English language and based on relatively small samples. When rigorous analyses were applied to "large and representative sets of personality-descriptive adjectives from many diverse languages" (p. 340), they suggested six personality dimensions, and used the acronym HEXACO as the naming convention for these dimensions: Honesty-Humility (H), Emotionality (E), Extraversion (X), Agreeableness versus Anger (A), Conscientiousness (C), and Openness to Experience (O).

The 3M Model

The Big Five and the HEXACO models highlighted before sought to relate personality traits to human behaviour in general. However, Mowen and Spears (1999) identified a hierarchical personality model for explaining consumer behaviour, more specifically.

Mowen and Spears (1999) developed a model which has antecedents in the work of Eysenck (1951), who demonstrated a four-level hierarchical model, naming the levels—Specific Response Level, Habitual Response Level, Trait Level, and Type Level, listed based on an increasing order of abstraction, with the lower level being the more tangible and visible than the higher ones.

The first level, Specific Response, which is at the lowest level of abstraction and the highest level of tangibility, represents the behaviour of the individual which may occur occasionally, in response to everyday situations which may not be characteristic of that individual despite displaying this behaviour. At the second level, Habitual Response, refers to a particular experience which is then repeated at another point in time, generating a similar response to each situation, thus displaying repetitive behaviour. The Trait Level is the third level on Eysenck's hierarchy, and these traits represent groupings of different habitual responses, building on the second level. Thus, individuals with the same groups of traits may respond similarly to the same circumstances. At the highest level of abstraction, we have the Type Level, where traits which are represented at the third level, are grouped into combined traits which represent the least tangible behaviour such as introversion or neuroticism.

Building on the concept of a hierarchical model used by Eysenck (1951), Mowen and Spears (1999) proposed a three-level hierarchical model of personality traits. Subsequent to the adoption of a three-level hierarchical model by Mowen and Spears (1999), Mowen (2000) conducted a series of studies and determined that the optimal hierarchical model should have four levels. The use of the four-level hierarchy by Mowen (2000) was supported by the earlier work conducted by Paunonen (1998).

In developing the four-level hierarchical model, Mowen (2000) highlighted two important issues with the three-level model by Mowen and Spears (1999). The first issue was related to the naming convention, where cardinal, central, and surface were the classifications used to identify the traits at the various levels in the hierarchy. Since Mowen (2000) found it difficult to determine a precise meaning of these classifications, he thought it best to derive new terms. The other issue that Mowen (2000) found concerned the number of levels in the hierarchy proposed by Mowen and Spears (1999), which had three hierarchical levels—cardinal traits, central traits, and surface traits, and Mowen (2000) found that these levels did not provide a comprehensive representation of the personality trait typology. He then developed four levels, in response to this shortcoming. These are elemental traits, compound traits, situational traits, and surface traits.

Elemental Traits—Mowen (2000) chose the term "elemental" to describe the basic traits as they were thought to be primarily derived from genetics and the learning environment to which the individual was exposed soon after birth. Mowen (2000) thought that these elemental traits were the fundamental factors that differentiated one individual from another, and in his model, these basic traits are combined to form other higher-level compound traits. In this model the eight elemental traits identified are: openness to experience, conscientiousness, extraversion, agreeability, neuroticism/instability, material needs, arousal needs, and physical needs.

Compound Traits—Compound traits are at the next level of the Mowen (2000) hierarchy. Compound traits are developed from elemental traits, as well as from the culture of the environment, and the learning experiences by the individual as a child. Mowen (2000) believed that there may be several compound traits in existence, some of which include: The need for activity, task orientation, the need for learning, competitiveness, the need for play, and effectance motivation.

Situational Traits—At the next level of the Mowen (2000) hierarchy are the situational traits, which are the interaction of elemental traits, combined traits and a specific situation, which produces a particular action by the individual. The Situational traits are therefore very specific, and may be observable in the sphere of consumer behaviour. Situational traits include: health motivation, impulsive buying, sports interest, value consciousness, and frugality.

Surface Traits—At the fourth level of the hierarchy, there are the Surface Traits, which are based on a combination of the situational traits, elemental traits, and compound traits. Surface traits are expressed as more tangible behaviours, and so they can more easily be observed than the other traits. Mowen (2000) provided examples of these traits, which include compulsive buying, healthy diet lifestyles, sports participation, modest living, bargaining, coupon proneness, consumer ethnocentrism, and consumer innovativeness.

The main goal of Mowen's (2000) research was to propose a model that would account for the stable nature of a person's inherent character or typical action taken for a given situation. The 3M model demonstrates the complex nature of the interactions among the traits depicted at the various levels in the model. These traits in combination influence the values and goals of the consumer (Mowen 2000).

BRIDGING PERSONALITY TRAITS AND CONSUMER TRAITS

Consumer traits may be said to be the same as personality traits operating within the narrow domain of the person acting as a consumer. Some research-ers use the basic personality factors from the Big Five Model and opera-tionalize them as consumer traits (Steenkamp and Maydeu-Olivares 2015; Otero-López and Villardefrancos 2013; Duhachek and Iacobucci 2005). Indeed, consumer traits are entrenched into the more basic personality traits (Joachimsthaler and Lastovicka 1984; Lastovicka 1982; Raju 1980). How-ever, the personality traits are generally at a higher level of abstraction than consumer traits (Lastovicka 1982). The Big Five is one of the most popularly used standardized personality trait models. However, the literature has not presented consumer traits in standardised models, and many of the basic personality traits are used as consumer traits in some studies (Steenkamp and Maydeu-Olivares 2015). In addition, Steenkamp and Maydeu-Olivares (2015) proposed a model to bridge the gap between basic personality traits and consumer traits by utilizing the factors in the Big Five Model and associating specific sets of consumer traits to each of the five factors. In this model, Openness was associated with consumer innovativeness, exploratory information search, brand loyalty, and store loyalty; Conscientiousness was associated with quality consciousness, price consciousness, and deal proneness; Extraversion was associated with market mavenism; Agreeableness was associated with susceptibility to normative influences and attitudes towards advertising, and Neuroticism was associated with impulsive buying. A longitudinal study carried out by Steenkamp and Maydeu-Olivares (2015) found that consumer traits demonstrate high stability, nearly as stable over time as the basic personality traits. This makes consumer traits enduring and effective in explaining buyer behavioural outcomes such as compulsive buying.

CONSUMER TRAITS AND
COMPULSIVE BUYING BEHAVIOUR

We are now at the stage where we can look at the specific relationship between consumer traits and compulsive buying behaviour.

Goldsmith, Flynn, and Goldsmith (2015) suggested that there are many psychological reasons that may be causal to compulsive buying. In addition, there are a wide range of non-psychological antecedents of compulsive buying (Shoham, Gavish, and Segev 2014). Researchers seem to agree that at a general level, consumers appear to engage in compulsive buying to alleviate some negative emotional state (Faber and O'Guinn 2008; Elliott 1994; Baumeister and Vohs 2007a), while others show a relationship between compulsive buying and external causes (Roberts and Pirog 2004; Chinomona 2013). For example, Chinomona (2013) indicated that compulsive buying behaviour may be caused by social and other external factors such as brand advertisement. He also found that the consumer traits of brand satisfaction, brand trust, and brand attachment were related to compulsive buying.

CLOSING COMMENTS

This chapter presented a brief review of the personality construct and addressed the development of personality traits highlighting the relationship between personality traits and consumer traits. It also introduced the association between consumer traits and compulsive buying and sets the stage for the predictive model that is developed in chapter 3 using the tenets of the 3M Personality Model.

Chapter Three

A Consumer Trait Model for Predicting Compulsive Buying

INTRODUCTION

This chapter is aimed at developing a predictive model that utilizes consumer traits for identifying key drivers of compulsive buying. Predictive models are probabilistic in design and utilize data and probability statistics to forecast expected outcomes. These models are constituted by several predictor (independent) variables mapped to one or more predicted (dependent) outcomes. The relationship between predictor and predicted variables are computed by statistical techniques such as multiple linear regressions, structural equations modelling, and neural networks. It is felt that the identification of drivers of this shopping behaviour is a necessary step in understanding this complex behavioural problem.

The empirical testing and results and discussion generated from the model developed are also presented in the chapter. Notably, the detailed discussions on the statistical technique of structural equations modelling (SEM) that was used for developing this model could make the chapter difficult to read and so the technical language is simplified, and complex tables and statistics are placed in the appendices for an easy navigation of the chapter.

Predictive models that utilize personality traits have already been used in the literature to identify and explain compulsive buying behaviours. For example, Mueller et al. (2010) and Otero-Lopez and Villardefrancos (2013) have addressed the personality trait predictors of compulsive buying with emphasis on the Big 5 personality traits—openness, conscientiousness, extraversion, agreeableness, and neuroticism.

Notably, most of the work in this stream of research have incorporated the Big 5 typology as the personality trait platform for addressing compulsive buying behaviour. However, for a better and more general understanding of consumer behaviour, more work is needed to address myriad personality traits, particularly those consumption-related traits that impact buying behaviour (Mowen 2000). On this basis, therefore, this model for relating consumer traits to compulsive buying was added to the literature in response to this gap. Moreover, more work on consumption-related traits will help with a more *layman-like* understanding of this complex shopping behaviour—a problem that has become so pervasive in modern societies.

WHY DO WE LINK CONSUMER TRAITS TO COMPULSIVE BUYING?

The predisposition of compulsive buying is seen as a consumer trait as it represents a consistent pattern of individual differences applied to the consumer. Some consumer traits are useful in predicting other traits based on the precepts of the Meta-theoretic Model of Motivation and Personality (3M Theory) advanced by Mowen (2000). This theory purports that personality traits are arranged through a hierarchal model of integrated traits where the lower order traits are known to predict trait-like behaviours of the same or of a higher order in the hierarchy (Mowen and Spears 1999). Moreover, higher order traits are also good indicators for predicting other higher order traits. The personality trait hierarchy consists of four levels and are arranged from the lower order elemental traits through compound and situational traits to the higher order surface traits (Fang and Mowen 2009).

Elemental traits, such as neuroticism and extraversion, lie at the base of the hierarchy and arise from genetics and early learning history (Mowen 2000). The traits of neuroticism ('tense' and 'irritable') and extraversion ('sociable' and 'energetic'), for example, provide a basis for predicting that these two traits, combined, could lead a young man to easily get into an argument with the cashier, speaking at the top of his voice, in the supermarket over a relatively simple matter.

Compound traits such as competitiveness and task orientation are second-level characteristics that result from combining elemental traits with the individual's learning history and culture (Mowen 2000). The traits of competitiveness ('go-getting' and 'assertiveness') combined with task orientation ('practical' and 'hands-on'), for example, could influence the individual, so predisposed, to request detailed hardware specifications on the computer he is purchasing and demanding features from the vendor at no extra cost.

Situational traits, such as rudeness, are third-level traits that are generated by the situational context; they result from the combination of elemental and compound traits (Mowen 2000). The situational trait of rudeness ('crudity' and 'bluntness'), for example, could explain why the individual, so predisposed, is only likely to be rude in situations where that individual is spoken to loudly by the attendant when shopping.

Surface traits, such as compulsive buying, are the highest order and most tangible traits in the hierarhy and emerge from the interaction of elemental, compound, and situational traits, and occur through product interactions (Mowen 2000). For example, the elemental trait of neuroticism could trigger the compound trait of need for recognition which could further interact with the situational trait of impulsiveness which could drive an individual to buy compulsively.

The model proposed in this undertaking is, therefore, a good fit for the 3M Theory (traits predicting traits) as it seeks to utilize a theorized set of consumer traits for predicting the surface trait of compulsive buying. These predictor consumer traits will be identified in the model development section next.

DEVELOPMENT OF A CONSUMER TRAITS MODEL

In developing the consumer personality model for predicting compulsive buying, a review of literature was undertaken to identify the possible consumer traits that are likely to be associated with this negative buying behaviour. This review, on each of the paths of association, is by no means exhaustive as the intention is to identify the theorized drivers of compulsive buying for the parsimonious development of the model.

Extensive literature on the theorized drivers of association in building empirical models is not available in many cases and so it is sufficient to develop a hunch or a cursory discourse for hypotheses building from the available literature. Indeed, if comprehensive literature were available on each of the theorized associations, it would hardly be necessary to develop models as this could suggest that the findings from new models are already known. This undertaking will, therefore, present a brief review of literature on the drivers of compulsive buying to set the stage for hypotheses building.

REVIEW OF LITERATURE

The review of literature resulted in at least twelve possible consumption-related traits that could be incorporated into the research model. These are encapsulated in Table 3.1.

Table 3.1. Consumer Trait Drivers of Compulsive Buying

1. emotional instability	7. vanity
2. consumer impulsiveness	8. materialism
3. extraversion	9. openness to new experience
4. status consumption	10. self-esteem
5. consumer need for uniqueness	11. conscientiousness
6. credit card misuse	12. agreeableness

Emotional Instability and Compulsive Buying

The emotional unstable or neurotic type personality is an individual who frequently demonstrates negative emotional states such as anxiety and depressive moods. These characteristically anxious, depressive, and self-conscious individuals often utilize shopping to mitigate their negative emotional moods. In this light, a long stream of researchers (Andreassen et al. 2013; Mikolajczak-Degrauwe et al. 2012; Thompson and Prendergast 2015) have associated this emotionally unstable behaviour with addictive shopping. For example, Shehzadi et al. (2016) found that neuroticism, facilitated by the trait of impulsivity among apparel customers, was a key driver of compulsive buying among these customers. Based on prior work, therefore, it is being hypothesized that emotional instability is a key driver of compulsive buying.

Consumer Impulsiveness and Compulsive Buying

Consumer impulsiveness is a predisposition that is characterized by the tendency to act without forethought, thus making quick decisions and failing to think of the circumstances beyond the here and now (Barratt 1993). This behaviour can be described as a sudden and immediate purchase of goods with no pre-purchase intentions (Beatty and Ferrell 1998). This spontaneous or sudden desire to buy something immediately can also be described as a struggle between the psychological forces of desire and willpower (Hoch and Loewenstein 1991) and viewed as more of an emotional than a rational response (Rook 1987). In the retail business, products are often classified into impulse and non-impulse purchases and marketing strategies are crafted to address each group.

It is important to differentiate between impulsive and compulsive buying behaviours as these two behaviours are closely linked. Impulsive buying connotes the spontaneous and unplanned buying behaviour while compulsive buying relates to the addictive and uncontrollable state of buying (Darrat et al. 2016). Bighiu et al. (2015) compare impulsive and compulsive buying:

Impulsive buying is the purchase triggered by external stimuli—for example, when waiting in line at the cashier register and see an item that you did not think of buying and suddenly add to your shopping cart. In contrast, compulsive buying is the desire to buy that comes from an internal force, such as the feeling of anxiety, with which the individual wants a relief, and therefore buys to feel calmer and happier. Prior research on the link between consumer impulsiveness and compulsive buying has provided strong support for the association between the two states.

For instance, Darrat et al. (2016) found that impulsive buying increases anxiety, which, in turn, drives compulsive buying. Similarly, de Paula et al. (2015) found a moderate association between impulsivity and compulsive buying and noted that other recent studies have indicated that impulsivity and compulsivity might represent a continuum. Based on prior research, therefore, it is being hypothesized that consumer impulsiveness is a key driver of compulsive buying.

Extraversion and Compulsive Buying

A consumer with an extraversion personality trait is characteristically outgoing and one who thrives on excitement. During the early stages of the COVID-19 pandemic, Dammeyer (2020), through exploratory analysis, found that extra shopping for stockpiling goods was associated with the extraversion trait. It appears that many of these shoppers were compulsive buyers who were found to be more extroverted than non-compulsive buyers (Mikołajczak-Degrauwe et al. 2012). The extraversion trait was also positively associated with several compulsive type behaviours such as Facebook addiction, exercise addiction, mobile phone addiction, and compulsive shopping (Andreassen et al. 2013). This link between extraversion and compulsive buying has also been corroborated by Ercis and Unalan (2017) who found that extraversion was a positive driver of compulsive buying tendency. Based on the foregoing, it is being hypothesized that extraversion is a key driver of compulsive buying.

Status Consumption and Compulsive Buying

Status consumption is the buying process by which an individual seeks to improve social standing through conspicuous consumption of goods and services that evoke status. This is described as a kind of power that invokes respect, consideration, and envy from people within the culture (Csikszentmihalyi and Rochberg-Halton 1981). Status consumption and materialism are very fundamental to consumer culture with compulsive buying being a negative by-product of this culture (Roberts 2000). The purchase of high fashion clothing, for example, is a manifest example of status consumption (Park and Burns 2005). Since fashion enthusiasts are likely to have compulsive buying tendencies (Park and Burns 2005), status consumption, in some shape or form, is expected to drive compulsive buying. More directly, Roberts (2000) found that status consumption was moderately correlated with compulsive buying tendencies. Based on the foregoing, therefore, it is being hypothesized that status consumption will positively drive compulsive buying.

Consumer Need for Uniqueness and Compulsive Buying

The evidence for a direct link between need for uniqueness and compulsive buying is, at best, sparse in the existing literature. However, Rajamma et al. (2010) found that consumer need for uniqueness provides a strong influence on the retail patronage behaviours of the millennial generation. This generation is notorious for online shopping which provides an increased sense of freedom for the shopper (Wolfinbarger and Gilly 2001). This sense of freedom may influence impulsive and compulsive buying behaviours among this group (LaRose and Eastin 2002). With limited evidence for a theorized relationship between need for uniqueness and compulsive buying, it is being hypothesized that need for uniqueness may be a key driver of compulsive buying.

Credit Card Misuse and Compulsive Buying

The wide availability and aggressive marketing of credit cards to college students is perhaps responsible for the high levels of compulsive buying among these students (Benson, Dittmar, and Wolfsohn 2010). Many researchers have found an association between credit card usage and compulsive buying. For instance, Roberts (1998) found that compulsive buying among college students was positively correlated with both the number of credit cards owned and the irrational usage of these cards. These findings suggest that the more credit cards owned, and the more injudicious usage of these cards are more likely to increase the compulsive buying tendency than less cards and better usage by the cardholder. Similarly, Park and Burns (2005) found that many people who had considerable interest in fashion were compulsive buyers and that credit card usage was a key driver of this behaviour among the fashion interests. In addition, Sari and Suyasa (2017) found that credit card usage was one indicator for predicting compulsive clothing buying among young women and that the materialistic nature of many of these young women was a better predictor of compulsive clothing buying than credit card usage. Based on the foregoing, therefore, it is being hypothesized that credit card misuse is a key driver of compulsive buying.

Vanity and Compulsive Buying

There are two main dimensions of vanity—physical appearance (e.g., fashion models who always want to look good) and achievement of success (e.g., purchase of expensive things to feel and give the appearance of success). The consumer trait of vanity is known to have a strong influence on consumer buying behaviour as the vanity inclined is always emotionally driven by physical appearances (Netemeyer, Burton, and Lichtenstein 1995). Many products such as cosmetics and clothing are marketed on a vanity appeal for targeting the vanity-driven segments of the market (Solomon 1992). The link between vanity and compulsive buying is, however, under researched despite the expected impact of vanity on buying behaviour. Ahmed et al. (2014) are among the few researchers who addressed this concern and found that vanity had a direct impact on compulsive buying of both university students and teachers. This means that the higher the levels of the vanity traits found among the group, the higher is the likelihood that these people would be more compulsive in buying habits. The impact of vanity on compulsive buying is expected to be similar across other samples and so with this limited evidence it is being hypothesized that vanity may be a key driver of compulsive buying.

Materialism and Compulsive Buying

Materialistic individuals are those who place material possession and physical comfort at the centre of their lives. In studying the association between materialism and compulsive buying, Pham, Yap, and Dowling (2012) found that highly materialistic consumers with poor financial management practices were particularly susceptible to compulsive buying behaviours. These results were corroborated by Donnelly et al. (2013) who found a direct relationship between materialism and compulsive buying and that poor money management was a trigger for the materialistic personality to buy compulsively. The path from materialism to compulsive buying is often very complex. This was demonstrated by Pradhan, Israel, and Jena (2018) who found that materialism was a key driver of credit card usage and use of the credit card increased the propensity for impulsive buying, which then precipitated the compulsive buying habits. On the basis of the foregoing, therefore, it is being hypothesized that materialism is a key driver of compulsive buying.

Openness to New Experience and Compulsive Buying

Openness to new experience is a consumer trait characterized by a preference for variety, intellectual curiosity and simply trying new things. The openness trait is found to be a positive predictor of both impulsive and compulsive buying (Gohary and Hanzaee 2014). This association was supported by Shehzadi et al. (2016) who found that the openness to new experience trait was positively correlated with compulsive buying. Moreover, Otero-López and Villardefrancos (2013) found that people who were open to new experiences and were materialistic were also likely to be excessive buyers. Based on the foregoing, therefore, it is being hypothesized that openness to new experiences is a key driver of compulsive buying.

Self-Esteem and Compulsive Buying

Self-esteem is a measure of an individual's self-worth and positively demonstrated by confidence and respect that that individual develops in his- or herself. Negative self-esteem is known for its association with excessive consumption as consumers will presumably shop for enhancing self-worthiness (O'Guinn and Faber 1989; Christenson et al. 1994). Hanley and Wilhelm (1992) also found that compulsive buyers had lower self-esteem compared with non-compulsive buyers. More recently, Adamcyzk, Capetillo-Ponce, and Szczygielski (2020), having examined numerous studies conducted across countries such as Canada, Germany, Poland, South Korea, and Hungary, found consistency across these countries in the negative correlation between self-esteem and compulsive buying. The literature is, therefore, indicating that negative self-esteem could be associated with compulsive buying across various populations and contexts. Thus, it is being hypothesized that low levels of self-esteem will drive high levels of compulsive buying.

Conscientiousness and Compulsive Buying

The conscientious consumer is one who is organized, responsible, persistent, hardworking, and motivated towards the attainment of one's goals (Piroth, Ritter, and Rueger-Muck 2020). Mowen and Spears (1999) found that more conscientious consumers were less likely to exhibit compulsive buying behaviour than the less conscientious ones. This inverse relationship between conscientiousness and compulsive buying has, more recently, been supported by Ercis and Unalan (2017) who found a similar negative association. Hence, the conscientious personality type is less likely to buy compulsively because conscientiousness characterizes the responsible individual who, expectedly, will take less chances with risky shopping (Shehzadi et al. 2016). Based on the foregoing, it is being hypothesized that low levels of conscientiousness will drive high levels of compulsive buying.

Agreeableness and Compulsive Buying

The agreeable personality is one that is characteristically kind, considerate, sympathetic and cooperative. Mowen and Spears (1999) found that there was a positive relationship between agreeableness and compulsive buying. Moreover, the agreeable personality type with an impulsive buying disposition is also likely to exhibit compulsive buying tendencies (Shehzadi et al. 2016). This positive association between compulsive buying and agreeableness was supported by Mikołajczak-Degrauwe et al. (2012) who found that compulsive buyers were significantly more agreeable than non-compulsive buyers. Still Mikołajczak-Degrauwe et al. (2012) argue that the positive association between agreeableness and compulsive buying were contrary to their expectations as chief among the motive of the agreeable individual is to maintain positive relations with others through socially desirable behaviours and compulsive buying behaviour would run counter to the agreeable personality. On balance, therefore, it is being hypothesized that agreeableness is a positive driver of compulsive buying.

PRELIMINARY STAGE OF MODEL TESTING

This review of literature was followed up by a preliminary stage of model testing to determine which of the consumer traits would be best fitted to the research model. This test was decided upon as the initial look at the items[1] that made up the consumer trait constructs[2] indicates that there could be multicollinearity[3] issues as some of these constructs such as status consumption, vanity and materialism had underlying items that were similar across the constructs. That is, some of the items that were used to measure status consumption were similar to those used to measure vanity and materialism— there being likenesses in the description of these consumer traits.

The Variance Inflation Factor (VIF)[4] was, therefore, used to test the levels of multicollinearity among the constructs; and all constructs with VIF values of 5 and higher were dropped as this indicated a potential for multicollinearity. See Hair, Ringle, and Sarstedt (2011) for details on dropping constructs when exposed to multicollinearity. Notably, the options available for fixing the constructs with multicollinearity issues are to merge the items of the constructs that are related or to remove the problematic constructs. Merging of these constructs was not the best option in this case as consumer trait constructs are distinct and so there would be a distortion in the meaning of a consumer trait construct if it were to be merged with another construct.

On analysis of the VIF data, only six consumer traits were found to be suited for inclusion in the research model. These are consumer impulsiveness, status consumption, consumer need for uniqueness, credit card misuse, vanity, and emotional instability. These traits were then utilized in the process of model development and further testing.

CONSTRUCTS OF THE REDUCED MODEL

The reduced model consists of six input constructs (consumer impulsiveness, status consumption, consumer need for uniqueness, credit card misuse, vanity, and emotional instability) and one output (compulsive buying). These constructs and associated items that were utilized in the reduced model are described below.

Consumer impulsiveness—Consumer impulsiveness as the process of buying without forethought and characterized by the scale items depicted in Table 3.2 that were developed by Puri (1996) and utilized in this study.

Table 3.2.   Consumer Impulsiveness Scale Items

impulsive	restrained (R)
careless	easily tempted
self-controlled (R)	rational
extravagant	enjoy spending
farsighted (R)	planner (R)
responsible (R)	

Status consumption—Status consumption is the process by which people strive to improve their social standing through conspicuous consumption of products and services that confer or symbolize status (Eastman, Goldsmith, and Flynn 1999). The Eastman, Goldsmith, and Flynn (1999) scale of status consumption that was utilized in this study consists of the items listed in Table 3.3.

Table 3.3.   Status Consumption Scale Items

buy product with status
interest in new product with status
pay more for product with status
product status is irrelevant (R)
place value on snob appeal

Consumer need for uniqueness—Consumer need for uniqueness is described as the quest by the consumer for differentness; and to do so by acquiring goods and services that will accentuate personal and social status. The scale on consumer need for uniqueness utilized in this study was developed by Tian, Bearden, and Hunter (2001) and consisted of the items depicted in Table 3.4.

Table 3.4. Consumer Need for Uniqueness Scale Items

collect unusual products/brands to be different
sometimes dared to be different in dressing in ways that others are likely to disapprove
lose interest in product/brand when it becomes popular
break customs and rules in product/brand purchase and situation in which it is used
purchased unusual products/brands to create a more distinctive personal image
purchase one-of-a-kind products/brands to create own style
avoid products/brands that have been accepted and purchased by the average
  consumer

Credit card misuse—Credit card misuse is the inappropriate usage of the credit card which usually results in excessive spending and out of control debt. The credit card misuse scale developed by Roberts and Jones (2001) was utilized in this study and consists of the items shown in Table 3.5.

Table 3.5. Credit Card Misuse Scale Items

less concerned with price when using card	take cash advance on card
exceed credit limit	spend more with card
pay off card monthly (R)	make minimum payment
impulsive when shopping with card	card regularly at maximum credit limit
too many cards	one card pays another
worry about card debt	delinquent on payment

Vanity—Vanity is seen as an excessive admiration of one's own self and appearance. The vanity scale utilized in this undertaking was developed by Netemeyer, Burton, and Lichtenstein (1995) and consisted of the attributes depicted in Table 3.6.

Table 3.6. Vanity Scale Items

the look of self is extremely important
very concerned with self-appearance
important to always look good
believe people notice how attractive they are
believe people are envious of their good looks
believe their body is sexually appealing

Emotional instability—Emotional instability, also referred to as neuroticism, characterizes an individual who displays excessive anxiety, oversensitivity, tension and obsessiveness. The scale on emotional instability utilized in this study was developed by Mowen (2000) and consisted of the items listed in Table 3.7.

Table 3.7.   Emotional Instability Scale Items

typically, moodier than others
temperamental (overemotional)
testy (easily irritated)
emotions go way up and down

Compulsive buying—Compulsive buying is an obsessive and uncontrollable urge to shop and usually results in the purchase of expensive or unwanted things. The scale developed by Valence, d'Astous, and Fortier (1998) was utilized in this study and consisted of the items shown in Table 3.8.

Table 3.8.   Compulsive Buying Scale Items

when have money, cannot help but to spend part or all of it
often impulsive in buying behaviour
have an irresistible urge to go into a shop to buy something
often buy product not needed, while knowing very little money left

Based on this scientific inquiry on the relationship between consumer traits and compulsive buying, six hypotheses were developed for testing the predictive model (Figure 3.1).

METHOD

The study on the predictive model utilized survey data that was collected over a two-month period using self-administered questionnaires.[5] The survey method was chosen as it is believed to be the most cost-effective way to collect data on consumer traits and buying habits from a wide cross-section of consumers. Moreover, the survey provides a feasible way of capturing quantitative data that are required for predictive models.

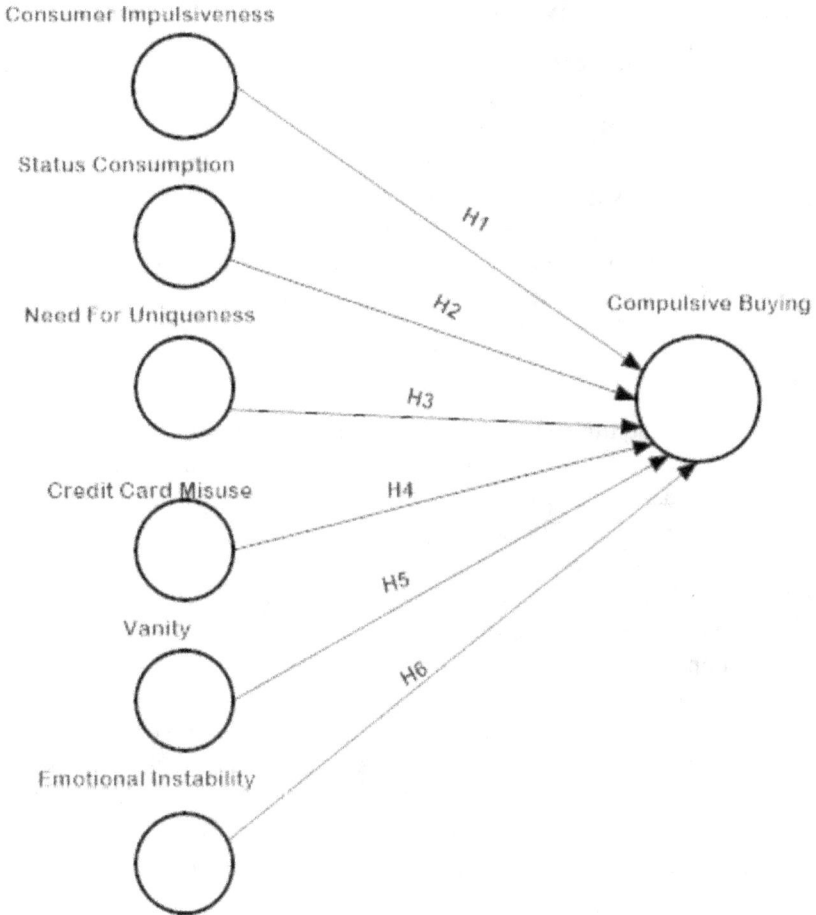

Figure 3.1. Theorized Drivers of Compulsive Buying.
Created by the authors.

Survey Instrument Development

The survey instrument consisted of the twelve predictor traits scales that were identified from the review of the literature, the compulsive buying scale and a set of demographic questions (gender, marital status, age, last level of educational attainment, and occupation) that were included for describing the sample. The items of each of these scales were measured using five-point Likert scales anchored from strongly disagree through to strongly agree. See Appendix 1 on the features tab of the book's web page for an excerpt of the survey instrument that relates to the final model.

Measurement Model Validation

Measurement models are utilized in statistics to validate the robustness, i.e., accuracy and consistency, of predictive models. This measurement model[6] of seven constructs and their underlying items (questions on the survey instrument that make up the constructs) was validated using Structural Equations Modelling (SEM) with SmartPLS 3. The results from the measurement model indicated that the model was robust and therefore appropriate for testing the theorized relationship model. See Appendix 2 on the features tab of the book's web page for validation of measurement model.[7]

Sample

The survey was administered to a convenience sample and participants were assured of anonymity and confidentiality. This resulted in a usable sample of 175 respondents. The final sample size of 175 was adequate based on the minimum sample size of 75 suggested for running this model of six input and one output constructs for attaining statistical power of 80 percent with significant level of 5 percent. See Hair et al. (2014, 21) for Cohen's recommended sample size in PLS-SEM models.

This sample was comprised of 53 percent females and 47 percent males. Fifty-eight percent of the respondents were single, 33 percent were married, and the other 9 percent were either separated or divorced. Over 34 percent of the sample were ages 25–30, 37 percent, ages 31–40, approximately 18 percent, ages 41–50, and the remaining 11 percent were over 50 years old. Most of these respondents (90 percent) were graduates of tertiary institutions; with professionals comprising 47 percent of sample, clerical and support workers, 27 percent and managers, 20 percent. See Table 3.9.

DATA ANALYSIS AND FINDINGS

Structural Equations Modelling (SEM) with SmartPLS 3 was used for assessing the relationship model. This technique was chosen for generating the relationships because of its no distributional assumptions, ease of handling complex models, ability to minimize unexplained variances and ability to test relationships between unobserved latent constructs[8] from observed items[9] that underlie these constructs (Hair et al. 2014). With this versatility, SEM is endorsed by the rated journals in marketing and psychology for testing predictive models.

In the relationship model, the six input constructs (consumer impulsiveness, status consumption, consumer need for uniqueness, credit card misuse,

Table 3.9. Descriptive Statistics on Survey Sample

Variables	Frequency	Percent	Cumulative Percent
Gender			
Male	60	46.9	46.9
Female	68	53.1	100.0
Total	**128**	**100.0**	
Marital Status			
Single	89	57.8	57.8
Married	50	32.5	90.3
Separated	9	5.8	96.1
Divorced	5	3.2	99.3
Widowed	1	0.7	100.0
Total	**154**	**100.0**	
Age			
25-30	57	34.5	34.5
31-40	61	37.0	71.5
41-50	29	17.6	89.1
51-60	13	7.9	97.0
Over 60	5	3.0	100.0
Total	**165**	**100.0**	
Last Level of Educational Attainment			
Primary	2	1.2	1.2
Secondary	15	8.8	10.0
Tertiary	153	90.0	100.0
Total	**170**	**100.0**	
Occupation			
Professional	45	44.6	44.6
Clerical & Support Workers	27	26.7	71.3
Manager	20	19.8	91.1
Other	9	8.9	100.0
Total	**101**	**100.0**	

vanity, and emotional instability) were mapped to the output construct of compulsive buying based on the Meta-Theoretic Model of Motivation and Personality (3M Theory) advanced by Mowen (2000). The 3M Theory suggests that consumer traits are linked through a hierarchical network of traits and that some traits can predict other traits at various levels within the hierarchy. Notably, compulsive buying is a consumer surface trait.

The results from this model showed that the six predictor constructs explained 41 percent of the variances observed in the outcome construct of compulsive buying. Four hypotheses were supported and the other two were not supported. Hence, consumer impulsiveness ($\beta = 0.221$; $p \leq 0.01$),[10] credit card misuse ($\beta = 0.295$; $p \leq 0.01$), vanity ($\beta = 0.147$; $p \leq 0.01$), and emotional instability ($\beta = 0.237$; $p \leq 0.01$) were positively associated with compulsive buying behaviour; thus, H_1, H_4, H_5, and H_6 were supported. No relationship was found on the impact of status consumption or need for uniqueness on compulsive buying behaviour, hence H_2 and H_3 were not supported. See Figure 3.2.

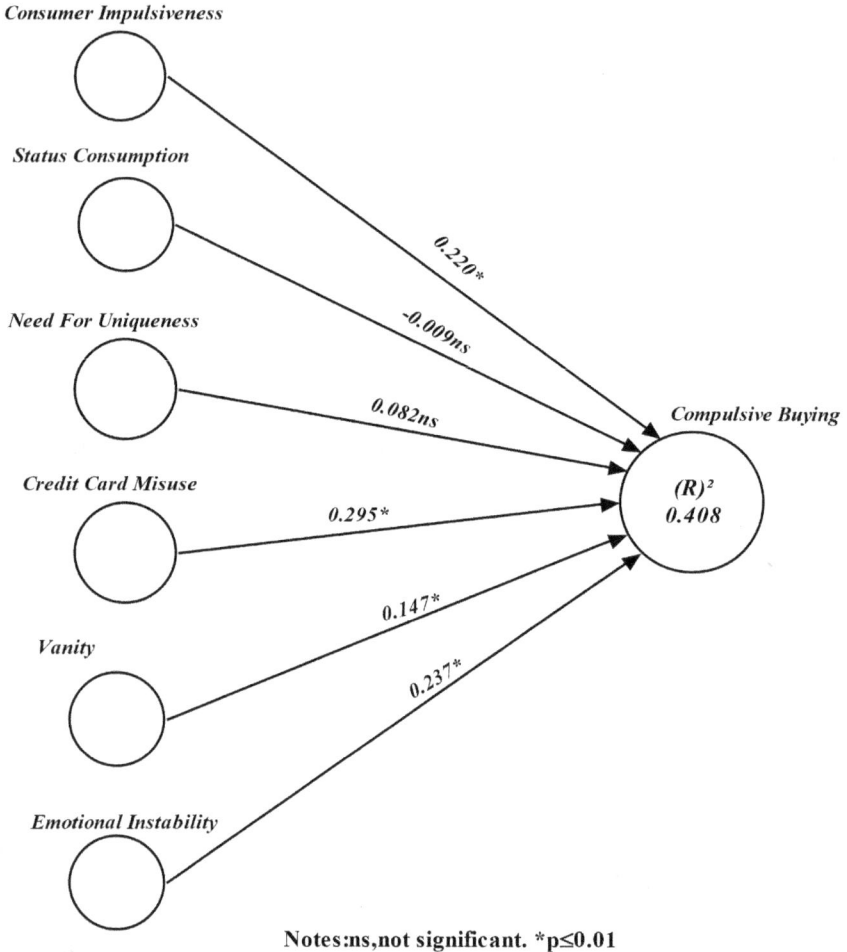

*Notes:ns,not significant. *p≤0.01*

Figure 3.2. Relationship Model of Consumer Traits and Compulsive Buying.
Created by the authors.

DISCUSSION AND IMPLICATIONS

This model of six consumer traits was quite successful in predicting the sur-face trait of compulsive buying as over 40 percent of the variance observed in compulsive buying was accounted for by these six constructs. Further, the 3M Theory provided a good fit for the model as all seven constructs in the model are trait-like with compulsive buying being representative of an out-come trait. The model also demonstrates that traits are effective in predicting associated traits—a basic tenet of the 3M Theory.

The study found that consumer impulsiveness, credit card misuse, vanity, and emotional instability were positive drivers of compulsive buying. These findings accord with expectations and indicate that all four consumer traits were strongly associated with compulsive buying with credit card misuse being the strongest. A more detailed discussion on these four triggers of compulsive buying ensues.

First, consumer impulsiveness is a quick and sudden response to an in-store stimuli while compulsive buying is an obsessive and addictive form of purchasing behaviour (Shoham and Makovec Brenčič 2003). These two states are strongly associated and seemingly lie on a continuum with compul-sive buying being the more troubling state. As such, people with tendencies of consumer impulsiveness are prime candidates for compulsive buying. These people can easily transition from the lower to the higher state through feelings of anxiety and depressive moods.

Second, credit card misuse lies at the epicentre of compulsive buying based on this study's findings. This misuse is facilitated by irrational use and owning multiple cards (Roberts 1998). These findings were similar to that of Omar et al. (2014) who found a positive link between compulsive buying and credit card misuse, and Joireman, Kees, and Sprott (2010) who found that consumers with higher compulsive tendency reported higher credit card debt. Notably, the credit card is perhaps the most serious threat to compulsive buy-ers and is therefore singled out for special treatment in this undertaking. See chapter 4 for a more detailed discussion on the credit card.

Third, the vanity inclined are materialistic, self-conscious, and people who are overly preoccupied with their own appearance. These people would, natu-rally, be interested in fashion and cosmetics (Solomon 1992) and are likely to be tempted by new designs and styles. Notably, Park and Burns (2005) found that individuals with an interest in fashion were often compulsive in buying behaviour. Despite the lack of prior research evidence on the associa-tion between vanity and consumer compulsion, in the general sense, vanity is believed to be a trigger for people who spend on high-end brands and is therefore expected to stimulate consumer compulsion as these personalities are known to impress and the more you think about impressing others, the more likely you will be compulsive and overspend.

Fourth, the positive finding on emotional instability is supported by a long stream of research (Andreassen et al. 2013; Mikolajczak-Degrauwe et al. 2012; Thompson and Prendergast 2015). These people are characteristically anxious and depressive and use shopping to generate an upbeat feeling. This neurotic type behaviour goes hand in hand with impulsivity (Shehzadi et al. 2016) and in combination provides further support for the association between neuroticism and compulsive consumption.

Contrary to our expectations, no evidence was found for associations between status consumption or need for uniqueness and compulsive buying. And so, while no scientific evidence is presented in this undertaking for linking these two consumer traits to compulsive buying, prior research has indicated that these traits could be triggers of negative consumption-type behaviours. See Roberts (2000) on status consumption and Rajamma et al. (2010) on the need for uniqueness. These two consumer traits should not be ignored in further undertakings on compulsive buying, despite their non-significance in this model, as there is research, albeit limited, and persuasive arguments, to suggest some semblance of association.

The intervention on compulsive buying must, therefore, take the four consumer traits of consumer impulsiveness, credit card misuse, vanity, and emotional instability into full consideration. This intervention should be executed through a process of self-regulation. The full discussion on the self-regulation of compulsive buying behaviour, taking into consideration the traits identified by this model, will be presented in chapter 5.

CLOSING COMMENTS

The model presented in this chapter provides support for Mowen's (2000) theory for using consumer traits at various levels of the hierarchy to predict other consumer traits—compulsive buying being the predicted trait. In this undertaking, each consumer trait was measured on a scale ranging from a low of 1 to a high of 5. This approach to measurement is consistent with the personality school of thought that suggests that everyone has all personality traits and individual differences are the result of the varying degree with which each person possesses these traits in combination. On this assumption, everyone has some level of each of the seven consumer traits, including compulsive buying tendencies, which were captured by this model.

The main inference from this study is that when shopping, which includes traditional, online, and window shopping, the individual who is impulsive, vanity predisposed, neurotic, or a misuser of the credit card is likely to exhibit compulsive buying behaviour, with or without shop stimuli, and this problem can be exacerbated or mitigated depending on conditional and situational contexts. Moreover, these negative consumption traits can generally be tempered through consumer intervention strategies which should be implemented through a process of self-regulation. The individual who finds him- or herself predisposed to any of these and related behaviours should therefore seek to self-regulate. See chapter 5 for details on the self-regulation process.

NOTES

1. Items are variables that make up the construct.
2. A construct is a combination of items.
3. Multicollinearity is a statistical condition that suggest that predictors are highly correlated with each other. This has the effect of making some predictors appear not to be significantly related to the predicted outcome when they are.
4. VIF is a statistical test that is used to determine if the predictors in a model are highly correlated.
5. Self-administration is a mode of administering surveys in which the respondents complete the questionnaires themselves.
6. A measurement model consists of constructs and related variables and is tested to ensure that the constructs and variables are both reliable, valid and robust.
7. A relationship model consists of the linking of constructs and variables in the model to test associations between constructs.
8. An unobserved latent construct is a theoretical conceptualization of the construct that cannot be observed directly and is measured by the items that underlie the construct.
9. Observed items are the variables within the model that are measured directly from the survey.
10. β represents the strength of the association between the consumer trait and compulsive buying. Positive β means that the association is positive; negative β means that the association is inverse. $p \leq 0.05$ means that the association is statistically significant.

Chapter Four

The Influence of the Credit Card on Compulsive Buying

INTRODUCTION

This chapter discusses the influence of the credit card on compulsive buying behaviour. It was empirically determined in this book project and corroborated by the existing literature that credit card misuse was a key driver of addictive shopping. The chapter is therefore aimed at exploring this relationship further. It also discusses the connection between marketing of the credit card by the issuer and its misuse by the cardholder. In chapter 3, we theorized that compulsive buying was dependent on a number of explanatory variables. These are consumer impulsiveness, status consumption, consumer need for uniqueness, credit card misuse, vanity and emotional instability. Four of these variables we found to be significant based on the predictive model that was tested: consumer impulsiveness, credit card misuse, vanity and emotional instability. We then concluded that these four consumer traits were key drivers of compulsive buying. Of the four significant drivers, credit card misuse was found to be the strongest and consequently the credit card was singled out for special treatment in this chapter.

The credit card is an electronic payment system that provides a quick and convenient way to make a purchase. Each transaction has at least four parties involved—the card network, the card issuer, the acquirer, and the card holder (Mann 2006). The card network is the institution that provides the infrastructure for the use of the card and determines the merchants that can accept the card as payment. The card issuer is the company that issues the card and sends the regular bills to the customer. The acquirer is the institution that processes the credit card transactions and credits or debits the accounts of the relevant parties. The cardholder is the consumer who uses the credit card to pay for purchases.

The credit card is primarily different from other payment systems as it promotes greater willingness to spend, elicits weaker recollections of past credit expenses and provides an overvaluation of available funds (Awanis and Cui 2014). This overvaluation may cause the cardholder to spend more money than budgeted.

Customers are quicker to make a purchase when they spend with the credit card than when they spend with cash (Feinberg 1986). The card also facilitates effortless transactions as it allows the purchaser to complete a transaction quickly, easily and without much thought. Alternatively, if the shopper were to use cash to make the purchase then surprisingly the shopper's thought process gets much more complex as this involves a number of steps such as the extraction of the cash, the counting of the cash, and for the shopper to ensure that enough cash remains for other purchases. The credit card in comparison tends to reduce the pain that would occur when parting with cash and postpones the mental reconciliation that comes about with spending (Roberts and Jones 2001). Moreover, cash payment results in the immediate parting with money and invokes the pain of paying (Awanis and Cui 2014).

Paying by cheque also has its psychological barriers to spending when compared with the credit card. In this case, the act of writing the cheque requires the recording of the total amount of the payment in both words and figures by the customer, thus leaving an imprint of the expenditure on the customer's mind. This imprint on the mind may serve as a deterrent to incurring future expenditure (Soman 2001). On the contrary, this is not the case with the credit card as it only requires a pin, signature or tap on tendering with the amount spent often evading the sight and mind of the customer as it is quickly recorded by the merchant through entering the amount and swiping the card. The credit card is therefore the payment facility that is most susceptible to overspending. As such, the credit card was found to stimulate and promote excessive purchasing thus creating a trap for the imprudent shopper (Roberts and Jones 2001).

The success of the credit card is contingent on the freedom it affords the cardholder to charge and sometimes even overcharge without being obliged to have cash. Thus, by design, you spend now and pay later—a favourite feature of the large majority of cardholders. This makes for the ease of misuse of the facility, particularly among people who are struggling with personal finances.

This chapter continues with a discussion on the marketing of the credit card and then presents a brief overview on credit card misuse. The prior research on the link between credit card and compulsive buying is next discussed along with the insights drawn from the prior research. The chapter is then concluded with the final remarks.

MARKETING THE CREDIT CARD

After the stock market crash that precipitated the Great Depression in 1929, consumer loans became a good source of revenue for financial firms when the demand for commercial loans had dramatically declined (Wolters 2000). These consumer loans led to a significant increase in consumerism and the credit card was introduced as a means of making a purchase through borrowing money up to the limit of the card. The metal card, called the Charga-Plates, was introduced during the 1930s and the plastic card became popular in the 1950s with the advent of the Diner's card (Steele 2018). This period coincided with the increasing wealth of the middle class and a simultaneous waning of the economic uncertainties that had lingered after the war, with both of these phenomena contributing to a situation where nearly half of US households had credit accounts by the 1950s (Manning 2000). This credit card, which is currently referred to as plastic money, is what we continue to use today and has emerged as one of the main ways of paying for shopping items in modern societies.

Marketers then began to segment the market to identify the most profitable customers of the credit card business. These are the customers who carry high balances and only make minimum payments at the end of the month. One of the first credit card marketing initiatives was launched by the Bank of America in 1958 when over sixty thousand unsolicited credit cards were sent to customers in California (Manning 2000). The Visa and Mastercard emerged by 1970 (Wolters 2000). Credit card marketing has now gone global with the advances in technology and banks continue to be aggressive in the marketing of cards due to the lucrative profits that are being made from credit card customers.

One of the distinctive features of the credit card is that it allows the consumer to purchase items using future income. Consequently, it is no longer necessary to save towards the purchase of a car, a television, or any other consumer item. It is also fairly easy to acquire credit cards with the heightened promotion by credit card marketers. Notably, in 2015 alone, credit card marketers sent over three billion solicitation mails to potential credit card users (Bryan 2015). Marketers are able to obtain the credit reports for the prospects of their target groups and ascertain the buying practices and credit management behaviour of shoppers and then create solicitation packages that will attract these shoppers. Marketing representatives are also able to find prospective credit card customers through data mining of banking information held on the databases of banks (Li et al. 2010). Some of the attributes that are mined using association rules are monthly income, gender, marriage, education, occupation, rent/buy, family size, and expenses. With this data, the marketers are competing in customer analytics for uncovering insights on both prospective and existing credit card customers (Davenport 2006). More broadly, big data analytics has now become a part of the banking landscape and used in areas such as sentiment analysis, product cross selling and compliance management (Srivastava and Gopalkrishnan 2015).

Credit card users can be segmented into convenience users and revolvers (Perera, Dayanga, and Jayasuriya 2013). The convenience users are prudent in using the facility and will pay off their balances at the end of the month and therefore do not pay interest charges. The revolvers on the other hand are those who do not pay off the balances and end up paying excessive interest and charges, thus using the credit card as a financial loan facility. These revolvers will pay a fraction of the card balances on a monthly basis and therefore carry over the balance on their debt to subsequent months. The credit card market is also divided into three segments (Zhao, Zhao, and Song 2009).

- Segment 1 has less than 40 percent of customers who pay off their balances at the end of each month and incur no interest charges.
- Segment 2 has less than 5 percent of customers who will end up with a bad debt that has to be written off by the credit card companies.
- Segment 3 consist of approximately 60 percent of the customers who are known to the credit card companies as the revolvers.

In marketing to these segments, the banks will first identify the customer characteristics of each segment, then value the segment and craft promotional strategies that are aligned with each segment (Li et al. 2010). Valuing of the segment will assist the financial firm to ascertain the profit potential of these segments and the bank will then target the profitable segment or segments. Targeting is also based on the customer profile of the segments and banks will target those segments where there is customer profile alignment with their offering. Credit card marketers will, however, focus their targeting on the third segment, which consists of the revolvers, primarily because it has the greatest potential for profits. Compulsive buyers will more often than not end up in this third segment, if not in the second segment of bad debt customers, as their credit card debt will usually get out of control and then the cardholder will struggle to make the minimum payment or not pay at all.

Those customers who do not pay the entire balance on their credit card bill, the third segment, will end up paying significantly more interest because of the carry over balances. Credit card companies, typically, require only a minimum payment of 2 to 5 percent of the balance, so many customers tend to pay the minimum required amount which sometimes barely covers the interest charges (Soll, Keeney, and Larrick 2013). These consumers then roll over the remainder of the balance to subsequent months. Consequently, the shoppers who are least able to afford to spend are the ones that bring the most profits to credit card issuers. As Freeman (2013) noted, 80 percent of the profits made by credit card issuers are from interest and late fees, rather than from annual fees.

The credit card is widely known for the high cost of borrowing. Still, many cardholders are oblivious to compound interest calculations that are utilized in credit card financing (Soll, Keeney, and Larrick 2013). When credit card customers pay the minimum amount required, it takes exceedingly long to clear the debt. Besides, less than 40 percent of customers will pay off the card balance at the end of the month and so the other 60 percent will be saddled by high compounded interest rates (Zhao et al. 2009). Notably, the banks are not bothered by the minimalized attitudes to paying these cards as any delay by customers to pay off their balances will be seen as more profits for the credit card issuer.

Marketing of the credit card is focused on promoting the positive images of lifestyle benefits and success and obfuscating the negative consequences of the debt (Burton 2012). Credit card marketers tend to target young adults such as college students as one of the growth markets. In doing so, the banks might waive some of their important requirements such as credit history and minimal income. This bullish approach to the marketing of the credit cards is often described as predatory (Stadler 2012) and the young unsuspecting adults are the easy prey. Thus, marketing of the credit card to college students continues to be a topical concern among both academics and policymakers and has led to the question of the students' ability to use and manage this facility (Limbu 2017).

The credit card is considered to be a catalyst for increasing sales and associated with increase in the frequency of spending (Feinberg 1986), increase in the amount that is spent (Soll, Keeney, and Larrick 2013), and increase in the number of transactions done by the retailer (Roberts and Jones 2001). This makes the credit card a very attractive product line of the financial firm.

The marketers of the credit card have crafted three basic strategies to boost return on investments (ROI) of this product line (Dera 2018).

1. Engage with new cardholders early and often—Contacting the customer after the first forty-five days of opening the account, and at regular intervals, thereafter, to reinforce the value proposition and benefits of the card, is aimed at building strong cardholder relationships with the credit card provider.
2. Prioritize existing cardholders based on potential for incremental spend—customer lifetime value (CLV) models and recency, frequency, monetary (RFM) techniques are used to identify cardholders who are in the market for incremental spend. This group of customers could be targeted for bolstering the cash flows of the credit card business.

3. Align offers to encourage desired behaviour—Promotional offers (e.g., use and get offer for cardholders with low transaction activities or spend and get offer for low spend cardholders) are used to reward desired changes in cardholder behaviour. These desired changes are ultimately aimed at using the card more frequently and spending more money.

These strategies are focused on the firm's bottom line and are oriented towards relationship building and consumer behavioural changes. They are masterminded by marketers to get cardholders to increase their spending to bolster ROI in the credit card business. Other popular strategies utilized by credit card marketers are presented by Papadimitriou (2012).

1. Focus each product on a single consumer need—Focusing each value proposition on one clearly delineated sub-segment at a time will allow the marketer to better predict, understand, and monetise the sub-segments. For example, if the focus were on lucrative rewards and high interest rates simultaneously, then some customers would spend to get the reward, pay off their monthly balances and therefore pay no interest and still benefit from the reward. The bank, in this context, would lose money to incur cost to give the rewards and not collect interest payments. Alternatively, if each value were to be focused on one sub-segment such as the lucrative rewards sub-segment separately from the high interest rates sub-segment then there would be a market for each value proposition and therefore money can be made in each sub-segments.
2. Bring together marketing and underwriting—Since underwriting does the pricing of the credit card risk, working together will help the marketer to pitch the offer to each sub-segment commensurate with the risk. This will also provide marketing with the required information to tailor the price of the product to fit the pocket of the customer.
3. Offer secured cards—This allows the marketer access to a significant customer segment that may not have good credit. Moreover, there is no risk to the firm as the facility is secured and a price premium can still be charged since the customer may not easily get the facility elsewhere with the bad credit.
4. Appeal to former debit card users—Customers who have stopped using their debit cards have a tendency to migrate to credit cards as a natural progression. These former card customers are usually prospected by marketers with credit cards as a low hanging fruit since their personal information can be obtained from the bank's archives and buying be-haviours can be worked out from their spending patterns using the data analytics.

5. Leave no customer empty-handed—This is a catchall strategy as most banks will take the bullish approach and target every customer with a credit card. This mass market approach allows the bank to make the most out of every marketing dollar spent and is intended to drive customer revenues. The banks will also mitigate its risk by offering secured credit cards to the high-risk customers.

In the line of doing business, marketing strategies are essential for recruiting new cardholders and sustaining the cardholder base of the credit card issuer. However, credit card marketing strategies raise ethical concerns, particularly in relation to the service provided to vulnerable spenders such as shopaholics. This is a moot point as credit card providers are in business to make money and must strategize to compete and sustain its operations. This controversy continues as addictive shoppers are expected to misuse the facility, yet credit card marketers are very strident in targeting this group who are woefully challenged in managing their spending. These ethical considerations in marketing to compulsive buyers will be discussed, in detail, in chapter 6. The next section will present a brief discourse on the misuse of the credit card and also sets the stage for the prior research which relates credit card misuse to compulsive buying behaviour.

THE MISUSE OF THE CREDIT CARD

Credit card misuse is described as the excessive and injudicious spending when using the credit card (Palan et al. 2011; Sidoti and Devasagayam 2010). These misusers, shoppers who are less concerned with price, regularly exceed credit limits, have too many credit cards, make minimum payments, spend more when using the card, are regularly delinquent on payment and shop impulsively with these cards (Roberts and Jones 2001). Shoppers with low self-esteem may misuse their cards to buy expensive items that they believe could repair their self-worth, hence allowing them to feel good about themselves (Omar et al. 2014; Pettit and Sivanathan 2011). More generally, people who view material things as a source of prestige are likely to misuse their credit cards (Tokunaga 1993). The extent to which the shopper sees money as a source of power or prestige is also associated with credit card misuse (Palan et al. 2011). Not surprisingly, therefore, sensation seekers and other risk takers such as gamblers were found to misuse their credit cards (Worthy, Jonkman, and Blinn-Pike 2010).

This misuse is also associated with impulsive purchasing (Pirog and Roberts 2007) which has close resemblance to compulsive buying (Verplanken and Sato 2011). The in-depth association between credit card misuse and compulsive buying will be explored in the upcoming section of this chapter. Other consumer traits found among young credit card misusers are introversion, emotional instability, materialism, and need for arousal (Pirog and Roberts 2007). The misuse of credit cards by college students has resulted in increased levels of dropout rates and high levels of debt and was also found to be associated with addictive shopping behaviour (Palan et al. 2011). The risky credit behaviour by many college students was also found to be related to parental norms and the socioeconomic status of the household (Xiao et al. 2011). It is, therefore, not uncommon for the students who observe the parents engaging in risky spending behaviours to also do so, particularly if they have access to money.

Credit card misuse is one of the main causes of consumer bankruptcy (White 2007). One of the issues with the credit card is the psychological comfort that the consumer gets from spending when using the card and is therefore tempted to spend more with the credit card than with cash. As noted by Swift and Ander (2016, 899), "by its very nature, credit card use creates the mirage of having more while paying less." This therefore facilitates cardholders in excessive spending to buy more items in the belief that they are getting a deal and not taking into consideration the full price of the goods which will take effect at the end of the period. Many customers are aware of the consequences of misusing the credit card but continue to do so and accommodate more debt because of diminishing financial stability and low self-regulatory capabilities (Awanis and Cui 2014).

The minimum payment per month that many cardholders make is in itself an act of misuse. In this situation, the cardholders are at a serious disadvantage as they make the purchase and the minimum payment is usually small compared with the outstanding balance on the card. Payment of the minimum amount will lead to astronomical interest charges, making the credit card balance unmanageable, and often leading to delinquency over time. The total amount paid for the goods purchased is also much more than the initial sale price when the minimum payment is made. Paying more than necessary is usually associated with the lack of financial knowledge of cardholders (Cakarnis and D'Alessandro 2015; Robb 2011). This lack of financial knowledge was found to be one of the main reasons for credit card misuse among college students (Norvilitis et al. 2006).

In the final analysis, credit card misuse is attributed to the risky shopping behaviour that leads to excessively high balances on the credit facility (Zainudin, Mahdzan, and Yeap 2019). Credit card providers will however facilitate this misuse by the customers as this is a built-in marketing strategy designed to generate high profit margins for the firm. This matter however becomes untenable for the financial institution when the cardholder is becoming or has become delinquent on payment or no longer makes payments on the card. No doubt, high levels of delinquency will threaten the profitability position that the marketers had sought to establish in the first instance.

CREDIT CARDS AND
COMPULSIVE BUYING: THE PRIOR RESEARCH

People suffering from compulsive buying disorder have reported episodes of this addictive behaviour which they believe are triggered by the credit cards they have in their possession (Feinberg 1986; Roberts and Jones 2001). No doubt, the credit card poses significant risk to compulsive shoppers as it exacerbates the already inherent urge to shop (Feinberg 1986; Roberts and Jones 2001). Compulsive buyers tend to own more credit cards and abuse these cards more than the average customer (O'Guinn and Faber 1989; Roberts and Jones 2001). They also carry higher card balances and are not as sensitive to prices (Kellett and Bolton 2009; Harnish, Bridges, and Karelitz 2017). This financial naivety demonstrated by many cardholders (i.e., not being sensitive to price, carrying high balances, and not paying off balances at the end of the period) also serves as a trigger for compulsive consumption (Lea, Webley, and Walker 1995).

Many researchers have reported significant relationships between credit card usage and compulsive buying behaviour (Lo and Harvey 2011; Norum 2008; Omar et al. 2014; Park and Burns 2005; Phau and Woo 2008; Veludo-de-Oliveira et al. 2014; Rashid et al. 2019; Roberts and Jones 2001). However, Khare (2013) found, contrary to popular expectations, that consumer attitudes towards the credit card was not related to addictive shopping.

The prior research in this stream of work are summarized below and the discourse is central to the association between credit card and compulsive buying and the variables that intervene or confound this relationship. Other aspects of the studies presented that were not relevant to this link or did not affect the association were not addressed in these discussions.

Omar et al. (2014): Compulsive Buying and Credit Card Misuse among Credit Card Holders—The Roles of Self-Esteem, Materialism, Impulsive Buying, and Budget Constraint

Omar et al. (2014) examined compulsive buying as one of the factors that could influence credit card misuse in Klang Valley, Malaysia. This study was motivated partly by the Malaysian government's concern to reduce personal debt that was largely attributed to credit card usage. Further, there was the view that the credit card/compulsive buying association had been examined in the Western world and so there was need to address these concerns in the non-Western context. Omar et al. (2014) decided to theorize in the opposite direction to most of the research in this stream, i.e., from compulsive buying to credit card misuse, and found that credit card misuse was positively influenced by compulsive buying thus suggesting that compulsive buyers would likely misuse their credit cards as a central part of their addiction.

Khare (2013): Credit Card Use and Compulsive Buying Behaviour

This study addressed the association between credit card usage and compulsive buying behaviour among Indian consumers. Khare's study was motivated by the author's view that compulsiveness varies with cultural differences and could be different across countries. This view was earlier mooted by Roberts and Sepulveda (1999) who investigated the relationship between attitudes to money and compulsive buying among Mexicans and found that the compulsive buying scale designed by Faber and O'Guinn (1992) for the US market was not applicable to Mexico because of cultural differences. The finding from the study done in Mexico was similar to the Indian study as Khare (2013) found that Indian consumers differed from their Western counterparts on compulsive consumption and their attitudes to credit card usage was not related to compulsive buying behaviour.

Veludo-de-Oliveira et al. (2014): Effects of Credit Card Usage on Young Brazilians' Compulsive Buying

The purpose of this study was to assess the roles of credit card usage in money attitudes and compulsive buying behaviour within the Brazilian context. This research was undertaken in response to the gap in the literature vis-à-vis the intervening role of the credit card in the relationship between money attitude and compulsive buying. The results of this study showed that credit card misuse was significantly related to compulsive buying among shoppers with high levels of anxiety. However, credit card usage did not mediate the effect of price sensitivity on compulsive buying thus suggesting that the use of the credit card had nothing to do with the low levels of price sensitivity displayed among compulsive buyers. This latter finding is contrary to the general thinking in this stream of work.

Park and Burns (2005): Fashion Orientation, Credit Card Use, and Compulsive Buying

The purpose of this study was twofold: First, to uncover the relationship between interest in fashion and compulsive buying among South Korean women. Second, to determine if credit card usage had an intervening role in this relationship. This study came about at a time when the Korean consumer market was thought to be changing with the doors opening to the global economy. The *dark side* of shopping was taking root and Park (2003) raised the concern that fashion and the credit card were integral to this problem. The findings of Park and Burns (2005) revealed that interest in fashion not only influenced compulsive buying directly but also indirectly through credit card usage.

Rashid et al. (2019): Impact of Materialism on Impulsive Buying: Mediating Role of Credit Card Use and Brand Loyalty

The main purpose of this study was to investigate the relationship between materialism and impulsive buying among shoppers at the malls of Lahore, Pakistan. The paper also sought to assess credit card use as one of the intervening variables between materialism and impulsive purchase. Notably, impulsive purchase was viewed as the less extreme case of compulsive buying (Verplanken and Sato 2011). Consequently, the Rashid et al. (2019) study that discusses impulsivity is relevant to this stream. This study with Rashid and colleagues was partly motivated by the authors' view that Pakistan had become a materialistic society and the credit card was perhaps responsible for much of the unplanned buying. The finding of the study that is relevant in this context is that credit card usage mediates the relationship between materialism and impulsive buying; thus suggesting that materialism will trigger impulsive buying among shoppers with the aid of the credit card.

Roberts and Jones (2001): Money Attitudes, Credit Card Use, and Compulsive Buying among American College Students

This study investigated the impact of money attitudes and credit card usage on compulsive buying among American college students. It was partially motivated by the need for policy that would regulate the marketing of credit cards on college campuses. Money attitudes were modelled using three attributes identified by Yamauchi and Templer (1982).

1. Power-Prestige—where people scoring high on this factor used money to impress others and as a symbol of success

2. Distrust (Price Sensitivity)—where people scoring high on this factor were hesitant, suspicious and doubtful in situations involving money
3. Anxiety—where people scoring high on this factor see money as a source of anxiety as well a source of protection from anxiety.

The findings of this study were as follows.

1. The power-prestige factor was a significant driver of compulsive buying among high credit card users but not low credit card users.
2. The distrust factor significantly lowers compulsive buying among low credit card users and not among high credit card users.
3. The anxiety factor significantly raised compulsive buying among high credit card users but not low credit card users.

Taken together, the findings of Roberts and Jones (2001) have certainly nuanced this relationship between credit card misuse and compulsive consumption.

Norum (2008): The Role of Time Preference and Credit Card Usage in Compulsive Buying Behaviour

This study analysed compulsive buying behaviour using a model that tested sixteen predictor variables, including money attitudes, gender, income, and credit card usage, against the outcome variable of compulsive buying. The author argued that compulsive buying was analysed from biological, psychological, sociological, familial, and demographic perspectives and her contribution was to examine it from an economic perspective which had not yet been done up the point of the 2008 study. The Norum (2008) study was done with a sample of students from a major Midwest university in the United States. The findings revealed that credit card usage was the strongest of the positive drivers of this addictive behaviour. This finding is consistent with our model that was tested in chapter 3 of this book where credit card misuse was found to be the strongest of the four positive indicators of compulsive buying.

Phau and Woo (2008): Understanding Compulsive Buying Tendencies among Young Australians—The Roles of Money Attitude and Credit Card Usage

This study sought to investigate the impact of money attitudes and credit card usage on compulsive and non-compulsive buyers using a sample of young Australians. The authors indicated that this was "the first Australian study that examined money attitudes, credit card usage and compulsive behaviour" (p. 441) and therefore the study was needed to better understand the problem in a country where compulsive buying was pervasive. The salient findings of the study were that compulsive buyers had higher credit card usage tendencies than their non-compulsive counterparts.

Lo and Harvey (2011): Shopping without Pain: Compulsive Buying and the Effects of Credit Card Availability in Europe and the Far East

This study compared the East and the West on the compulsive buying/credit card dynamics. A sample of shoppers from Taiwan was used to represent the East and a similar sample from the United Kingdom represented the West. The findings were that compulsive shoppers across countries overspent and were rarely concerned about prices. This overspending was partially due to the excessive usage of the credit card. On the comparison of East and West, it was found that addictive shoppers were more compulsive in Taiwan than they were in the United Kingdom.

INSIGHTS FROM THE PRIOR RESEARCH

The prior research presented the scholarly work on the credit card / compulsive buying dynamics in a number of countries. The countries represented were the United States, India, Pakistan, Malaysia, Mexico, Brazil, South Korea, Australia, Taiwan, and United Kingdom. Jamaica was also represented as the primary research done in this book (and discussed in chapter 3) and utilized a sample that was drawn from Jamaican shoppers. With this international reach, the insights gained from the review of these studies are far-reaching.

First, and most fundamentally, both the literature and the primary research done for this book have signalled a causal relationship between credit card usage and compulsive buying across countries despite others, albeit in the very small minority, such as Khare (2013), who concluded that this general association of credit card and compulsive shopping may not hold in Eastern countries such as India as the shopping attitudes to credit card usage were not related to compulsive consumption. This matter was however viewed differently by others such as Lo and Harvey (2011) who found that overspending by compulsive shoppers from both Eastern and Western countries were partially attributed to the use of the credit card. Lo and Harvey (2011) also found that shoppers in the East were more compulsive than those in the West and this argument was later corroborated by studies that found that compulsive buying prevalence rates could be as high as 16.4 percent in the United Kingdom (Maccarrone-Eaglen and Schofield 2017), representing the West and 29.1 percent in China (He, Kukar-Kinney, and Ridgway 2018), representing the East.

Second, there appears to be interdependence between these two consumer traits of credit card misuse and compulsive buying, with Omar et al. (2014) theorizing in the opposite direction, and finding that compulsive buying was also a positive driver of credit card misuse i.e., the more you buy compulsively, the more likely are you to misuse your credit card. This argument on interdependence could find support in the 3M Theory that was advanced by Mowen (2000), and discussed in chapters 2 and 3, whereby a set of consumer traits are effective in predicting another set of consumer traits through a networked and interdependent arrangement of personality traits. Thus, we conclude that if you buy compulsively (a consumer trait) you are likely to misuse your credit card (another consumer trait) and conversely, if you misuse your credit card then you are also likely to buy compulsively.

Third, the relationship between credit card misuse and compulsive buying could still be confounding even with overwhelming support for the direct relationship. For example, credit card misuse could exacerbate compulsive buying among shoppers who display an anxiety disposition. Similarly, shopping for fashion clothing with the credit card may also invoke the compulsive buying behaviour of the shopper. Further, the materialistic trait could further influence compulsive buying among shoppers when the credit card is used as the means of payment.

Fourth, attitudes to money may also complicate the relationship between credit card misuse and compulsive buying. Here are three examples gleaned from the Roberts and Jones (2001) study that emphasises this point.

1. Shoppers who see money as a status symbol and are heavy users of the credit card are also likely to buy compulsively.
2. Shoppers who are price sensitive and are low credit card users are not likely to buy compulsively.
3. Shoppers who are price sensitive and are high credit card users are also likely to buy compulsively.

CLOSING COMMENTS

The chapter outlined the relationship between credit cards and compulsive buying behaviour in a discourse that is driven by the prior research. No doubt, there is good in owning and appropriately using the credit card. However, based on its ease of use and the ability to ignore, or at best delay the consequences of spending more than originally intended, or spending more than one has, the credit card can become a liability in the wrong hands. This is the case of the credit card in the hands of the compulsive buyer. Buyers with such a disorder demonstrate an inability to ignore urges to spend even when they can ill afford to do so. This problem is exacerbated by the shopping stimuli that are presented by credit card marketers.

One compelling reason for the strong association between credit card and compulsive shopping is that compulsive buyers are heavy users of the credit card and the more frequently they use these cards, the more they anticipate and actually engage in further usage (Hirschman 1979). Thus, the credit card lends itself to a kind of compulsivity and known for spontaneous spending (Mavri and Ioannou 2004). Moreover, spending with the credit card has been associated with financial problems among the general buying public (Kara, Kaynak, and Kucukemiroglu 1996) and therefore a *fait accompli* that compulsive buyers would have problems when spending with this facility.

We conclude that the aggressive marketing of the credit cards has markedly contributed to the misuse of this facility and high levels of misuse have contributed to compulsive buying. We are also suggesting that intervening variables such as anxiety, poor attitudes to money, and materialistic tendencies could also amplify this causal relationship between credit card misuse and compulsive buying.

Chapter Five

Self-Regulating Compulsive Buying Behaviour

INTRODUCTION

This chapter addresses self-regulation in general terms while making the connection with compulsive buying behaviour. It is felt that a general understanding of self-regulation could help the compulsive buyer to exercise the necessary control for curbing this behaviour. The chapter begins with a background on self-regulation, makes reference to behavioural versus emotional self-regulation, and explains the real-world context that gives rise to the association between self-regulation and compulsive buying.

The chapter discusses, further, a theoretical framework for explaining self-regulation and highlights the prior research for relating self-regulation/self-control to impulsive/compulsive buying. Notably, and similar to Baumeister and Vohs (2018), the terms self-regulation and self-control are used interchangeably in this undertaking because of the near equivalence of terms. There is also demonstrable evidence of similarity, if not equivalence, with impulsive and compulsive buying in the context of self-regulation (Verplanken and Sato 2011), and, consequently, these behaviours were treated with likeness vis-a-vis self-regulation.

The chapter also presents a conceptual model, that was developed by the authors of this book, for explaining the linkages between self-regulation and compulsive buying behaviour. In addition, strategies for self-regulating consumer traits that drive compulsive buying behaviour were discussed in this chapter.

There has been a relentless effort in the psychological sciences for improved understanding of the underlying processes of self-regulation with the great significance that it plays in modern life (Eisenberg et al. 2019). Further understanding of this human behavioural process is also required as it is fundamental to better consumer decision choices (Baumeister and Vohs 2018). These choices are presented in all spheres of life, not least of which include consumer markets and so a self-regulation approach is essential for curbing consumption and maintaining a balance in life. This makes the study of self-regulating compulsive buying behaviour both relevant and topical given the pervasive nature of the shopping problem. Moreover, there is a paucity of work in the extant literature for linking self-regulation to compulsive buying despite the need for better understanding of this association.

BACKGROUND TO SELF-REGULATION

Philosophical questions are often asked as to why some people are better behaved, better organized, more punctual and have better shopping attitudes than others. And while the answers to these questions are complex and vary widely, many psychologists would agree that self-regulation is at least a part of the answer to these questions.

Self-regulation can be broadly defined as any effort by the human self to alter its inner state or responses (Vohs and Baumeister 2016). "The ability to control and regulate our actions is perhaps the quintessential character-istics of the human being" (Forgas et al. 2009, xi). Thus, self-regulation is the process by which the individual consciously controls his or her attitudes and behaviours through a feedback loop towards the attainment of goals or outcomes (Baumeister et al. 2006). This phenomenon requires discipline to resist temptations as the self-regulatory process involves an enduring pursuit of a sought-after goals (Mischel 1996). As such, self-regulation is facilitated by human motivation and willpower. Notably, the process of self-regulation has general and wide applicability to human behaviours and actions.

Self-regulation is an activity pursued by people to bring themselves in line with their desired goals (Fenton-O'Creevy, Dibb, and Furnham 2018). For example, people use budgets to self-regulate their spending impulses in order to save enough money to make purchases that are aligned with their long-term goals. This trait-like behaviour, that displays individual difference across people, is akin to self-discipline and used by top performers to distin-guish themselves from others. Importantly, self-regulation is fundamental to the control of all human behaviour and obviously not specific to compulsive buying behaviour.

The psychological concept of self-regulation is a human behavioural process that leads to positive life outcomes when effectively executed. This predisposition is necessary in all endeavours of life and people who do more self-regulating are likely to outperform those who do less. Through self-regulation, some people are better able to control their thoughts, feelings, emotions, and shopping behaviour than others. Thus, it is expected that people who actively regulate themselves, and have good self-control, will have fewer behavioural problems (e.g., smoking, drinking and compulsive buying), be less stressed, be happier, and enjoy a more fulfilling life (Baumeister and Vohs 2018). Moreover, almost all personal and social problems that affect people are associated with some kind of failure to self-regulate (Vohs and Baumeister 2016).

The ability to self-regulate is dependent on both personal characteristics and situational variables. In effect, some people in some situations are better able to self-regulate than other people in the same or other situations. Thus, the pursuit of self-regulation is a moving target. This cognitive process is also dependent on one's psychological capacity along with one's passion and desire.

The human trait of self-regulation is a highly adaptive predisposition that enables people to control and alter their behaviours to live up to social and ethical standards (Baumeister et al. 2006). This is the process by which the self intentionally alters its own response to thoughts, emotions, impulses, performance, and behaviours in order to meet the set standards (Baumeister and Vohs 2018). These standards include rules, goals, norms, ideals, and plans. Through this adaptive process, an individual will actively self-regulate to maximize gains from a given situation (Mithaug 1993).

This human resource of self-regulation is also akin to strength or energy and is therefore limited in capacity (Muraven and Baumeister 2000). Since this trait has limited capacity, attempts at self-regulation will result in ego depletion (diminished self-regulatory resources, i.e., a kind of mental exhaustion), and further attempts could decrease the likelihood of success (Baumeister and Vohs 2007b). That is, self-regulation is likely to decline on current attempts after people exert self-control in a previous related or unrelated context (Baumeister 2018).

Self-regulation can, therefore, be likened to the muscle, and like the muscle, the process of self-regulation can be strengthened through exercise and practice (Baumeister et al. 2006). However, after expending energy to self-regulate, and similar to exerting energy to work the muscle, after people exercise self-control for a protracted period, they are less willing or able to muster up further self-control towards the attainment of their goals (Baumeister and Vohs 2018). That said, there is enough academic evidence that suggests that an individual can be effectively trained for improving their self-regulatory capabilities (Muraven, Baumeister, and Tice 1999; Oaten and Cheng 2007).

This phenomenon of self-regulation can be applied across a wide expanse of human life. This includes food consumption, healthy lifestyle, personal finance, and a wide range of psychological issues such as low self-esteem, anxiety, and compulsive shopping.

In applying self-regulation to food consumption, Petit et al. (2016) illustrated the psychological process undertaken by the health-conscious consumers on exposure to foods: Health-conscious consumers, when tempted by appetizing food, divert attention away from their senses (such as sight and smell) and from bodily states (such as arousal state and salivation), and keep in mind their long-term goal of losing or maintaining weight. The researchers explained the differences in self-regulating the senses versus the bodily states from their research findings: Ongoing attempts at regulating these sensory cues of sight and smell in the decision choice would usually result in ego depletion (reduced strength and willpower), thus leading to unhealthy food choices. In contrast, self-regulating the bodily states of arousal and salivation may help the consumer to make healthier choices.

While acknowledging that self-regulating food consumption for attaining body weight goals is a complex psychological phenomenon, Petit et al. (2016) concluded that health-conscious consumers who self-regulate their behaviour towards their long-term goals, such as ideal body weight, while focusing on their bodily states of arousal and salivation, are more likely to make healthier food choices than those consumers who focus on the sensory queues of sight and smell. These findings on food consumption are suggesting that the trait of self-regulation has both psychological and physiological implications for controlling behaviour.

In the context of shopping behaviour, retail store designs and merchandising policies are intended to create an environment for influencing shopper reactions and actions towards the purchase of products (Babin and Darden 1995). Most consumers will find it difficult to walk by a store without enquiring or at least becoming curious in the shopping environment. These shopper responses are dependent on both individual characteristics and situational variables with the trait of self-regulation providing the means for regulating shopping impulses. The shopping environments will not have the same effect on all consumers, as some consumers are better able to self-regulate their emotions and purchasing behaviours. No doubt, the process of self-regulation will aid the buyer to curtail buying impulses and become thrifty (Sohn and Choi 2012).

The compulsive buyer also has the difficulty to resist inner urges to shop excessively. This out-of-control shopping behaviour is done for relieving low moods and feelings and viewed as a chronic failure to self-regulate one's obsessive shopping behaviour (Faber and O'Guinn 1992). There are also variants of the self-regulatory behaviour that are relevant to the compulsive buyer. These include underregulating and mis-regulating of the buying behaviour. Underregulating refers to the failure to exert self-control and mis-regulating is the misguided directing of self-control away from the desired result (Baumeister and Heatherton 1996). These two behavioural distortions run counter to the positive goal of curbing compulsive buying behaviour. The next section discusses behavioural versus emotional self-regulation.

BEHAVIOURAL VERSUS EMOTIONAL SELF-REGULATION

To self-regulate is to control the things that we think, feel, say, and do in order to advance our goals and objectives. This predisposition is known to produce a sense of control over one's behaviours and emotions. Self-regulation can be addressed from both behavioural and emotional perspectives thereby allowing us to distinguish the regulation of our actions from our feelings.

Behavioural self-regulation is the ability of the individual to *act* in a manner that is consistent with his/her interest or in the interest of some other person(s). For instance, a man who may not want to buy groceries after work as he would like to watch the after-work game with friends but regulates his behaviour and shops in the interest of his wife and children, which does provide an example of behavioural self-regulation. Emotional self-regulation, on the other hand, is the ability to exercise control over emotions such as thoughts, feelings and moods in the interest of the individual or other party. For instance, a man who gets into an angry mood because of poor customer service from the corner shop owner and suddenly decides to calm down as he thinks to himself that despite the difficulty experienced, the store is so convenient for picking up snacks (when he is on the late shift at work) as comparable with the other shops that are too far away from his office. This latter scenario demonstrates a case of emotional self-regulation. Notably, behavioural self-regulation (Kingston 2015) and emotional self-regulation (Claes et al. 2010) are both applicable to the study of compulsive buying behaviour as consumer actions and feelings go hand-in-hand for a triangulated understanding of this shopping behaviour.

THEORETICAL FRAMEWORK
FOR EXPLAINING SELF-REGULATION

The process of self-regulation can be viewed from a number of theoretical frames. These include Social Cognitive Theory of Self Regulation (Bandura 1991), Self Regulation Theory (Baumeister and Vohs 2007b), and Regulatory Focus Theory (Higgins 1998). However, for best fit, Self Regulation Theory and Regulatory Focus Theory were chosen for shedding light on this phenomenon of self-regulation. Further, Regulatory Focus Theory (Verplanken and

Sato 2011) and Self Regulation Theory (Claes et al. 2010) were both associated with the study of compulsive buying, making these theories relevant in this undertaking.

Regulatory Focus Theory

The Regulatory Focus Theory provides a framework for explaining self-regulation. This theory purports that people are motivated towards the attainment of goals via two distinct self-regulatory orientations—promotion and prevention (Higgins 1998). The Regulatory Focus Theory assumes that in pursuit of goals, people are motivated towards pleasure, i.e., promotion orientated and away from pain, i.e., prevention oriented (Bryant 2009).

Brockner and Higgins (2001) explain that:

1. when people are promotion focused, they are motivated by growth and development needs thus bringing actual self or behaviour in alignment with ideal self through the standards they set and the aspirations they have to reach these standards; and
2. when people are prevention focused, they are responsive to security needs in which they align their actual selves with their *ought* selves thus setting standards based on assigned duties and responsibilities.

Similarly, Verplanken and Sato (2011) submit that:

1. promotion orientation involves the individual's pursuit to reach out for a desired outcome (e.g., accomplishments, growth, and aspiration) and regulates his/her behaviour towards the attainment of that outcome; and
2. prevention orientation involves the individual's effort to avoid a bad outcome (e.g., pain, losses, and failure) and regulates his/her behaviour to avoid punishment and negative outcome.

Self-regulation is, indeed, a dynamic state, and at a given point in time, people may practice self-regulation with either a promotion or prevention focus (Brockner, Higgins, and Low 2004). Moreover, promotion and prevention not only vary as a predisposition across individuals but can also be induced, based on the situational context (Higgins 2012).

Promotion orientation is associated with eagerness as a means of attaining goals while prevention orientation is associated with vigilance as a means of attaining these goals (Higgins 2002). Notably, the promotion/prevention dynamics provide two approaches towards the attainment of goals. However, both forms of orientation can propel the individual towards the same goal and the choice of orientation is merely dependent on individual predisposition and preference. In the case of consumer products, Higgins (2002) argues that promotion and prevention orientation are aligned with the value dimensions of the products. In contrasting the two orientations, he suggested that people who are promotion oriented will align with values such as luxury for reflecting accomplishments, and with technical innovation for signalling a state-of-the-art product. People who are prevention orientated, on the other hand, will align with values such as protection-warning for reflecting safety, and with other values such as reliability-service for reflecting security.

A Self-Regulation Theory

Self Regulation Theory purports the existence of a system of personal management that is responsible for consciously guiding one's own thoughts, feelings and behaviours towards the attainment of one's goals (Baumeister and Vohs 2007a). Baumeister, Heatherton, and Tice (1994), in an attempt to advance this strength model for self-regulating human behaviour, identified three ingredients that are essential, and which work in tandem in this self-regulatory process. These are standards, monitor, and willpower. In further research by Baumeister and Vohs (2007b) compelling evidence was found for the addition of motivation as the fourth ingredient of the framework. This was found to be essential as motivation is needed within the psychological frame to bolster the strength and limited resources in the self-regulation model. Thus, the individual sets standards for the desired behaviour, develops the motivation to meet these standards, monitors the thoughts and actions to make sure that the behaviour is aligned with the set standards, and musters up the willpower by developing internal strength and controlling urges in order to attain the desired outcome. The following provides a brief discussion on each of the four ingredients of self-regulation.

Standard—Standards in simple terms are ideas of how something should or should not be done, and include goals, norms, values, and expectations (Baumeister and Vohs 2016). These standards are targets and provide well-defined requirements for the behaviour that needs to be changed. The setting of standards is a necessary prerequisite for attaining the desired outcomes.

Motivation—Motivation refers to a general drive or inclination to do something (Baumeister and Vohs 2007b). It represents an inner drive to meet the standards that are set. This attribute can be bolstered through incentives such as compensation and recognition which, in effect, could help the individual to overcome ego depletion (Muraven and Slessareva 2003).

Monitor—Monitoring is an essential part of self-control and involves keeping track of one's performance on the standards that were set (Baumeister and Vohs 2016). This is a process of observing and checking one's progress, repeatedly, on the set standards for attaining the desired outcome. Monitoring requires the follow-up on one's behaviour (that is to be changed) via a feedback loop and altering one's behaviour, as necessary, to bring it in line with the set standards.

Willpower—Willpower is an exercise of one's internal energy and strength thereby controlling urges for attaining the desired outcome. Ego depletion is associated with willpower and is seen as a state of diminishing willpower occasioned by prior exertion of self-control (Baumeister 2014). Job et al. (2010), through a provocative study, found that the depletion effect in self-regulation could possibly be eliminated if people were to believe that their willpower was unlimited.

Even when standards are clearly established and one is motivated and monitoring is effectively executed by the individual, if one does not have the willpower to develop the inner strength, then one may still fail to self-regulate (Baumeister and Vohs 2007b). The next section will present a brief epistemological perspective for associating self-regulation with compulsive buying.

Self-Regulation Linked to Compulsive Buying through Theory

The link between self-regulation and compulsive buying is quite complex and should be addressed from a comprehensive and an epistemological perspective. However, in the interest of parsimony, this link will be explained through the Regulatory Focus Theory (Higgins 1998) and the Self Regulation Theory (Baumeister and Vohs 2007b).

Verplanken and Sato (2010), in applying the Regulatory Focus Theory to impulsive buying behaviour, and underscoring the complexity of consumer behaviour, indicated that the impulsive or compulsive buyer in the purchasing decision may either take a promotion orientation, in a search for pleasure, or a prevention orientation, to avoid feelings such as low self-esteem. Hence, the literature has signalled that the regulation of impulsive or compulsive buying behaviour can be viewed from both the promotion and prevention perspectives. Indeed, buying compulsively to satisfy one's materialistic values could be seen as a promotional orientation while buying compulsively to avoid fear or mood swings could be seen as being prevention focused orientation. Similar to Verplanken and Sato (2010), therefore, and consistent with the Regulatory Focus Theory (Higgins 1998), compulsive buying will be analysed in this undertaking from the perspective of the two identified orientations of promotion and prevention.

Compulsive buying can also be explained through the lens of the Self-Regulation Theory promulgated by Baumeister and Vohs (2007b). In this context, compulsive buyers can self-regulate to improve their shopping problems by setting standards for improving their addictive behaviour. They would then develop the necessary motivation to meet the behavioural standards and monitor their buying behaviour vis-à-vis these standards. It would also be necessary for the compulsive buyer to develop the required willpower to keep the behaviour in line with the desired outcome.

Equivalence of Self-Regulation and Self-Control

People often fail to regulate themselves because of the lack of self-control. In practice, the term self-regulation is used interchangeably with the term self-control. However, there is a slight difference between these two terms that must be highlighted. That is, self-control, in the strictest sense, represents the cognitive act of inhibiting impulses and emotions while self-regulation is more extensive and entails the cognitive and loop-like behaviour for reducing both intensity and frequency of those impulses and emotions (Shanker 2016). In effect, self-control can be viewed as an action while self-regulation, a process. Self-regulation is, therefore, the more far-reaching of the two behavioural states since to control the behaviour it may first be required to self-regulate through practice. Notably, the endgame of self-regulation and self-control is to modify or maintain a desired behaviour. Due to the closeness in these terms therefore and similar to Baumeister and Vohs (2018), these two terms will be used interchangeably in this undertaking.

Equivalence of Impulsive and Compulsive Buying in a Self-Regulation Context

Compulsive buying is classified as qualitatively distinct from impulsive buying (Faber and O'Guinn 2008). However, at a glance, compulsive buying may be viewed as an extreme case of impulsive buying (Verplanken and Sato 2011). In fact, Faber (2004) argued that compulsive buying should be classified as an impulse control disorder in the DSM.

The resemblance between these two consumption traits is supported by a few studies which have found that both behaviours are linked to materialism and identity concerns (DeSarbo and Edwards 1996; Dittmar, Long, and Bond 2007) and to lack of conscientiousness and openness to experience (Mowen and Spears 1999; Verplanken and Herabadi 2001).

Impulsive buying occurs as a part of a wider psychological functioning and is considered to be a trait that aligns with self-regulatory behaviour (Verplanken and Sato 2011). Notably, both impulsive and compulsive buying behaviours are associated with self-regulatory activities (Fenton-O'Creevy, Dibb, and Furnham 2018; Vohs, Baumeister, and Tice 2008b).

The failure to control many addictive behaviours, such as compulsive buying, may be attributed to the lack of self-regulation and control (Vohs and
Baumeister 2016). Similarly, impulsive buying can be viewed as a failure
to self-regulate (Fenton-O'Creevy, Dibb, and Furnham 2018; Verplanken
and Sato 2011). Both impulsive and compulsive buying are triggered when
there is conflict in the shopper's motivation, i.e., to buy or not to buy. Given
the closeness of the terms and similarity in practical applications of the two
behaviours vis-à-vis self-regulation, this project will also treat these terms
with likeness.

Prior Research on Self-Regulation/Self-Control Linked to Impulsive/Compulsive Buying

The existing literature is sparse on studies that have addressed the relationship between self-regulation/self-control and impulsive/compulsive buying
behaviour. There is also evidence to suggest that both self-regulation/self-
control and impulsive/compulsive buying are often used interchangeably in
this stream of work. After all, the strategies to self-regulate or self-control
impulsive/compulsive buying would hardly be different in a real and practical
sense. In this undertaking therefore, these terms are used with equivalency in
explicating this link. Notwithstanding the paucity of research for establish-
ing this link, a few studies have addressed this relationship and left us with
some practical insights and implications. These studies are presented next in
a logical, and not a chronological sequence, for easy ordering of the findings.

First, Achtziger et al. (2015), in studying the link between self-control,
compulsive buying and consumer debt, found that self-control was negatively
related to consumer debt and compulsive buying was positively related to
these debts. This means, *ceteris paribus*, that consumers with less motivation
to self-control are expected to have more debt than those consumers with
more motivation to control themselves. Similarly, these findings, as expected,
also suggested that compulsive buyers are expected to have more consumption debts than non-compulsive buyers. Among other things, the findings of
this study attested to the importance of self-control in mitigating compulsive
buying behaviour.

Second, Xu et al. (2020), in a more recent study, found that self-control
was negatively associated with the consumers' urge to buy impulsively online
and negatively associated with the consumers' actual impulse to buy online.
These findings again provide support for self-control as a tool for addressing
maladaptive buying behaviour and suggest that self-control is essential for
mitigating the urge to buy impulsively online and for preventing the actual
impulsive online purchase.

Third, Claes et al. (2010) found that compulsive buyers displayed low
levels of effortful control, i.e., low levels of ability to regulate emotions and

behaviours, even after controlling for depressive symptoms. This means that compulsive buyers will display low levels of self-regulation in their purchasing behaviours even when they are not experiencing mood swings and low self-esteem issues. This finding is a bit surprising as it was expected that these maladaptive shoppers would only buy excessively when they were experiencing depressive moods.

Fourth, Vohs and Faber (2003) conducted two experiments in a study on self-regulation and impulsive spending patterns. In experiment 1, they found that participants who displayed lower levels of self-regulatory resources were more impulsive in buying styles than those with more regulatory resources. Similarly, in experiment 2, it was found that participants with less regulatory resources generally indicated that they would pay more for high priced products when compared to those participants who had more self-regulatory resources. These findings suggest that the more self-regulatory ability and willpower that the individual has, the less impulsivity/compulsivity that he or she will display in shopping behaviour. The results also suggest that consumers who are lower in self-regulation will pay more money for high-priced products than those consumers who are high in self-regulation.

Fifth, Sultan, Joireman, and Sprott (2012), in exploring whether simple physical and cognitive exercises, practiced over a two-week period, can reduce consumers' urges to engage in impulsive buying, found that both repeated physical and cognitive self-control exercises were impactful in reducing this buying behaviour. It is believed that the strengthening of the individual's self-control will lead to the reduction in buying tendencies (see Lades 2014). Thus, failure in self-control tends to increase compulsive spending (Black 2007). Baumeister et al. (1994) also referred to the state of behavioural snowballing i.e., the breakdown in effort to self-regulate—a state that is typical of the compulsive buyer.

Sixth, Sohn and Choi (2012), in a qualitative assessment, encapsulated the findings on compulsive buyers who were actively going through a process of self-regulation.

- They accepted their addictive shopping problem.
- They attempted to block or confront the problem of excessive shopping.
- They disposed of their credit cards.
- They abstained from watching TV to avoid advertisements that triggered their impulsivity.
- They limited the usage of the internet to avoid internet shopping.
- Some attempted to reengage in interpersonal relationships.
- Some channelled energy into physical activities such as yoga and travel.
- Some became more disciplined about shopping, making shopping lists and maintaining daily journals.
- Others began to pursue religious activities.

Seventh, Baumeister (2002) explained that the act of self-control in consumption may fail in instances when:

- there is conflict of goals, e.g., to buy a personal item or to save the money towards the payment of a utility bill;
- people stop monitoring their behaviours, e.g., the shopper makes the purchase without checking the budget to see if the item can be afforded; and
- people are mentally exhausted, a state of ego depletion, e.g., the shopper is tired and exhausted from a rough day's work and makes the purchase without having the energy to rationalize the decision.

Making purchasing choices can also lead to mental health exhaustion and this may result in diminishing self-control, making shoppers more vulnerable to impulsive buying (Vohs et al. 2008a). In effect, self-control operates like a muscle (Baumeister et al. 1998) and just like the muscle, self-control can get fatigued with physical exertion and can also be strengthened over time through physical training (Sultan et al. 2012). That said, ongoing efforts at self-control will render a person weaker in subsequent attempts (Vohs and Faber 2003).

Taken together, the prior research in this area has indicated that self-regulating of one's behavioural predisposition should positively influence one's buying behaviour. There is also academic evidence to suggest that the trait of self-regulation is limited in capacity and can even be depleted through successive attempts at self-regulating. However, self-control can be bolstered through physical and cognitive self-control exercises. Further, prior research has offered a number of strategies for helping the compulsive buyer to improve upon buying behaviour. These include, acknowledging that the addictive behaviour is a problem for the individual, discarding of credit cards, avoiding television advertisement, monitoring of shopping behaviour and finding alternative preoccupations to shopping such as yoga, travel, and physical exercise. The next section presents a conceptual model for encapsulating and shedding further light on the relationship between self-regulation and compulsive buying.

A Conceptual Model for Linking Self-Regulation to Compulsive Buying

The buying situation experienced by the compulsive shopper is very complex as it involves a myriad of external and internal factors and forces. Any attempt therefore at explaining the situation faced by the compulsive buyer would be conceptual and extremely parsimonious, at best.

In attempting this monumental task, the authors of this book encapsulated the link between self-regulation and compulsive buying behaviour using the illustration highlighted in Figure 5.1.

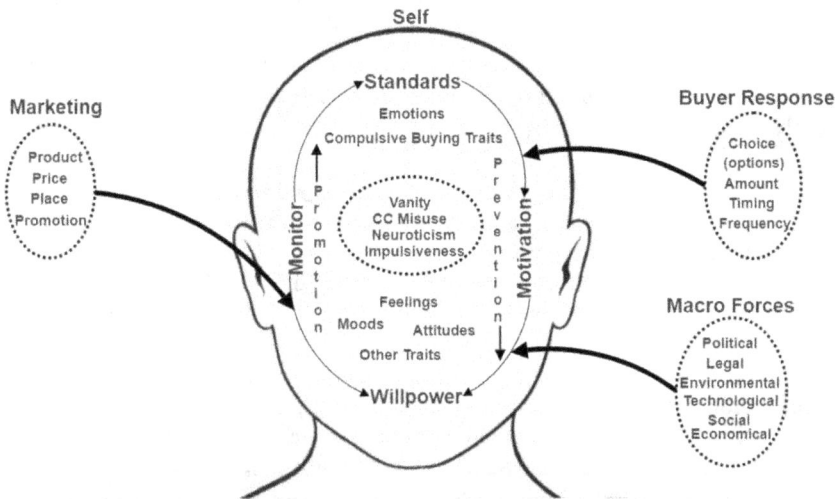

Self

Standards
Emotions
Compulsive Buying Traits

Marketing
Product
Price
Place
Promotion

Monitor
Promotion

Vanity
CC Misuse
Neuroticism
Impulsiveness

Prevention
Motivation

Buyer Response
Choice
(options)
Amount
Timing
Frequency

Feelings
Moods
Attitudes
Other Traits

Macro Forces
Political
Legal
Environmental
Technological
Social
Economical

Willpower

Figure 5.1. Self-Regulating Compulsive Buying Behaviour.
Created by the authors.

This schema is depicting that the compulsive shopper is faced with external forces (e.g., marketing stimuli, buyer response options and macro forces) and internal forces (e.g., moods, feelings, emotions, attitudes and consumer traits). Notably, consumer traits, such as vanity, credit card misuse, neuroticism and impulsiveness, which are drivers of compulsive buying, and highlighted in chapter 3, work in tandem with the other forces to confound compulsive buying behaviour and this behaviour can be mitigated by the general process of self-regulation.

This self-regulatory process in the context of compulsive buying can be explained from at least two theoretical perspectives—Regulatory Focus Theory (Higgins 1998) and Self Regulation Theory (Baumeister and Vohs 2007b). In conceptualizing this process, it is assumed that the compulsive buyer could be predisposed to either the promotion orientations or the prevention orientation or to both orientation in pursuit of the purchase (Higgins 1998). Further, this buyer is also predisposed to the feedback loop of setting standards, developing the motivation and willpower to meet these standards and monitoring the compulsive buying behaviour for attaining the desired results (Baumeister and Vohs 2007b).

In a practical sense, when faced with a compulsive shopping situation, one should first get a handle of one's buying orientation (promotion/prevention), taking into consideration the buying queues and forces, along with those associated predispositions (e.g., vanity, impulsiveness), and then self-regulate the buying situation through the feedback loop for achieving the desired outcome.

Self-regulating one's addictive shopping behaviour through the frame of Regulatory Force Theory and Self-Regulation Theory can be illustrated practically as follows:

A lady who is a shopaholic is currently displaying a depressive mood manifesting in low self-esteem and lack of self-confidence. She has the long-term goal of acquiring a house and currently has a low-paying job. This lady is currently shopping for groceries and suddenly spots a pair of shoes in the display of a nearby store. She is not in need of the shoes but buying shoes and clothing items provides her with retail therapy and usually helps her with her low mood. Wearing branded shoes, she believes, will also help her to look more accomplished as she is promotionally focused in her orientation. Despite her low self-esteem, she does not seek to be preventative in her behaviour i.e., ensuring that she has the budget to secure such a purchase and be more vigilant in her spending.

In preventing herself from purchasing the pair of shoes that is not needed, therefore, she must acknowledge that she is currently displaying a promotional tendency (need for accomplishment) and then rationalise this thought on its merit through self-talk—Do I really need to get this shoe for me to feel accomplished? In rationalizing this thought, she will more often than not conclude that the display of her promotional orientation in acquiring the shoes will not lead to a feeling of accomplishment in the long run and at best will provide a buyer's high for alleviating her depressive mood. Contemplating her buying decision therefore is a first step in mitigating addictive shopping. Notwithstanding the rationalizing of the decision to purchase the item, the lady should also self-regulate through the strength model to ensure that she does not relapse on her decision not to make the purchase. To do so, she must then set the standard for shopping for shoes, e.g., to buy shoes when needed and have a budget in place to do so. She should next develop the motivation and willpower to only buy when her standards are met and then constantly monitor her shopping behaviour to ensure that shopping for items does not take away from her long-term goal of acquiring the house in good time.

It must be stated that consumers who are prone to compulsive buying should never go shopping during a state of ego depletion (a temporary state of reduced capacity of self-control) that is often present when one is hungry or in a negative mood as they are in a state where they would not have the strength to resist addictive shopping (Achtziger et al. 2015). Needless to say, self-regulating compulsive buying behaviour is a complex problem and therefore cannot easily be explained. However, our attempt here is to simplify as much as practicable for a layman-like understanding of the link between self-regulation and compulsive buying behaviour.

Consumer Traits, Compulsive Buying, and Self-Regulation

There are many predispositions, internal to the consumer, including mood, attitudes, motivations, and traits that could influence the compulsive buyer. There are also external factors such as family and market influence that could drive compulsive buying behaviour. Again, compulsive buying is very complex and could be driven by so many factors that are both internal and external to the consumer. That said, there is consensus in extant literature which suggests that consumer traits provides a sizable part of the explanation for buying behavioural outcomes such as brand loyalty (Smith 2015), gambling activities (Fang and Mowen 2009), credit card misuse (Pirog and Roberts 2007), and negative consumption-based emotions (Mooradian and Olver 1997). It therefore becomes necessary to better understand the role that consumer traits play in this maladaptive buying behaviour and craft self-regulatory strategies for reducing the effect of traits on buying behaviour.

This undertaking, through its epistemological discourse in chapter 2 and empirical study in chapter 3, presented a deepening of the understanding of the role that consumer traits play in compulsive buying behaviour and identified the consumer traits of consumer impulsiveness, credit card misuse, vanity, and neuroticism as the key drivers of this behaviour. These negative consumption traits can be self-regulated for mitigating compulsive buying behaviour. The discussion that follows will, therefore, present the strategies for self-regulating these consumer traits.

STRATEGIES FOR SELF-REGULATING KEY CONSUMER TRAITS THAT DRIVE COMPULSIVE BUYING

For the impulsive consumer, possible self-regulation strategies (Ramsey 2019) could be as suggested next.

- Make a budget and stick to it—budgeting is essential for good money management.
- Give yourself slack to spend—create a line item in your budget for slack/money to spend the way you like.
- Sleep on the decision before you make a purchase—giving yourself a day to temper your impulse.

- Make a shopping plan—knowing what to buy and how much to spend will curb overspending.
- Beware of too many promotions sent by email—too many email blasts on coupons, free shipping and extra discounts will influence spending.
- Do not shop when you are in an emotional state—emotions should not dictate spending.
- Bring company with you when you shop—bringing a friend or sibling with you will help you to talk through shopping scenarios for better decision making.
- Use cash sometimes instead of card and take only the cash that you plan to spend—sticking to your shopping plan of using cash and not having extra money in your possession does not provide room for impulsive buying.
- Stop comparing yourself with others—try to be grateful for what you have instead.
- Keep your long-term goals in mind—giving in to impulse buying will not advance your goal whether the goal is to pay off your mortgage or get out of debt.

For credit card misusers, possible self-regulation strategies could include:

- reducing the numbers of credit card used;
- reducing limits on credit cards to amounts that can be cleared in full each month; and
- putting your card on hold with the provider during vulnerable periods such as when depressed or lonely or when there is an urge for shopping therapy.

For the *vanity predisposed*, the self-regulating strategies could include:

- reduced exposure to fashion and beauty magazines; and
- making less comparisons with others on physical appearance and achievements.

For the neurotic personality types, the intervention strategies could include the following.

- Joining self-help group, e.g., Debtors Anonymous, which should help to control neuroticism, which in turn will mitigate compulsive shopping, which tends to feed on itself and follow the same cycle as other forms of addiction such as alcoholism and gambling (Goleman 1991).
- Doing exercises for stress and anxiety which should help to curb neuroticism as this behaviour is manifested in stress and anxiety.
- Doing cognitive behaviour therapy for mitigating anxiety symptoms.

An attempt was made in this section to fit self-regulation strategies to the consumer trait types that were most impactful on compulsive buying based on the findings of the empirical study in chapter 3. However, it must be noted that most of these self-regulatory strategies are not unique to the consumer traits discussed here and may have applicability in mitigating compulsive buying behaviour more generally. Moreover, these self-regulatory interventions could also be utilized to curb other behavioural issues such as gambling and alcoholism. Further, consumer affairs groups and other stakeholders could also frame intervention strategies for assisting the shopaholic personality type from the mix of strategies presented in this undertaking.

Gollwitzer and Sheeran (2009), in a more generalized sense, proposed the if-then plans as a self-regulatory strategy for better consumer decision making. By using these plans (if situation X arises in my shopping experience, then I will show shopping behaviour Y), people can also navigate their emotions and thoughts through a process of self-talk for better shopping decisions.

CLOSING COMMENTS

This chapter presented a detailed discourse on self-regulation linked to compulsive buying behaviour drawing mainly on a Theory of Self Regulation conceptualized by Baumeister and Vohs (2007b) and the Regulatory Focus Theory advanced by Higgins (1998).

The limited prior research for exploring the link between self-regulation and compulsive buying were also explored for explicating this complex phenomenon. In addition, a conceptual model was presented in the chapter on the internal and external forces that drive compulsive buying behaviour and the process of self-regulation for mitigating this behaviour. Strategies for self-regulating consumer traits that drive compulsive buying were also discussed in this chapter as these traits were deemed to be a black box for linking self-regulation to compulsive buying. In the final analysis, a general approach to self-regulation is seen as an overarching strategy for mitigating compulsive buying behaviour. It was also concluded that identifying and applying self-regulatory strategies for preventing and coping with this buying behaviour is a must do if compulsive buyers are to mitigate this problem.

Chapter Six

The Ethical Considerations in Marketing to Compulsive Buyers

INTRODUCTION

In this chapter, the authors introduce a rationale for the discourse on ethical considerations in marketing to compulsive buyers. The chapter includes a brief discussion on ethics in marketing with highlights on the marketing mix and possible dilemmas faced by marketing managers. These discussions also address marketing and utilitarianism and present the philosophical argument that marketing actions are in pursuit of the *greater good* and may therefore be in conflict with service to smaller and vulnerable groups. Marketing management considerations in providing for compulsive buyers are discussed and a template for identifying compulsive buyers and tendencies is included. Central to the discussions in this chapter is the marketing to compulsive buyers on ethical grounds. In this context, marketing ethics is discussed vis-à-vis marketing to consumers with compulsive buying traits (credit card misusers, the vanity inclined, impulsive personalities and the neurotic type personality) and marketing to vulnerable segments such as women, children, and teenagers who are prone to compulsive buying tendencies. These discussions are concluded with a framework that utilizes prompting questions for assessing the ethical readiness of the firm for treating with customers who are prone to compulsive buying behaviour and tendencies. The chapter was included in the manuscript in response to the gap presented in both the psychology and marketing literature vis-à-vis paucity of work on the ethical considerations in marketing to vulnerable groups (see Gupta 2013, 45).

The principal aim of marketing is to capitalize on the needs of the customer and make a profit by serving and satisfying these needs. On this basis, the practice of marketing raises an ethical question on the role of marketing: Is marketing designed to exploit the vulnerability of customers that is presented through their physical and psychological needs? In answering this question, the socially responsible firm pursues ethical practices in service to its customers. Thus, ethics embody the guiding principles of the firm for carrying out the marketing activities responsibly.

The ethical approach to marketing can also be viewed as a corporate initiative to promote the firm since good ethical practice is expected to be met with the favourability of the customer who, in turn, would be loyal to the firm. Moreover, ethics in marketing continues to be a controversial topic since there has always been the conflict of making money while being socially responsible. Nonetheless, the socially responsible firm is now giving more attention to ethics in the practice of marketing and is no longer solely striving to maximize profits but is also seeking to ensure that marketing is practiced fairly and provides societal benefits for assisting vulnerable groups (Mikolajczak-Degrauwe and Brengman 2014). That said, marketing ethics do not go far enough in addressing the vulnerability of consumers on matters such as compulsive buying behaviour.

Compulsive shopping is a widespread societal problem that directly affects many people in the general shopping public. Recent studies have presented reported cases of 16.4 percent in the United Kingdom (Maccarrone-Eaglen and Schofield 2017) and 29.1 percent in China (He et al. 2018) with the prevalence rate varying from 1 to 8 percent worldwide (Weinstein et al. 2016).

There are several implications of compulsive buying for individuals so affected (Roberts 1998). First, the affected individual may not always be sensitive to the consequences of this action. For example, a husband with this problem may have financial difficulty in meeting his expenses due to over-spending and still does not curtail his shopaholic behaviour even though it is affecting his wife who now has to be spending more in the household and, in turn, cannot meet her budgeted expenses. Second, the compulsive buyer is affected by negative emotional states such as depression, frustration, and low self-esteem which certainly have implications for personal relationships and wellbeing. Third, the compulsive buyer is expected to be faced with out of control debt which has implications for the personal bankruptcy and embarrassment of the individual.

Roberts (1998) explained that compulsive buying could also have negative consequences on the natural environment due to the high levels of waste that result from excessive and unregulated buying. This waste is often caustic and therefore contributes to the depletion of the earth's resources. Thus, compulsive buying is not only a problem of the customer but also a problem of the firm as this dysfunctional buying behaviour could also hurt the brand reputation of the firm, in the long run, if the customer were to associate the societal problems believed to be caused by compulsive buying with the marketing actions of the firm (Japutra, Ekinci, and Simkin 2019).

The marketer can also be viewed as an active partner in the psychological problems that are experienced by compulsive buyers since marketing is designed to create the urge in the customer to make the purchase. This urge is generated through advertising, promotion, and shopping stimuli and consequently the compulsive shopper will get out of control with spending to satisfy that euphoric feeling associated with shopping. For Gupta (2013), "enticing sales, attractive in-store displays, attention giving sales personnel and easy credit might all promote compulsive buying" (p. 45).

As indicated earlier, this association between marketing practice and compulsive buying will raise many ethical questions such as: "Are marketers taking advantage of vulnerable consumer populations by designing practices or techniques that accrue benefits for the company at the expense of exploiting vulnerable populations?" (Gupta 2013, 46). This therefore becomes a matter of philosophy as the marketer grapples with the question on what aspect of the marketing practice is right and what aspect is wrong.

ETHICS IN MARKETING

One of the basic takeaways from business school is that success in business is represented by increased revenues and profits. This has led to a dog-eat-dog business culture among some marketing practitioners with little regard for the moral side of doing business. Marketing is the business function that connects closely with the customer and so good ethical practices on the part of the marketer has become important to the discerning firm. Moreover, good ethical practices are necessary for developing customer commitment and trust. And, commitment and trust are key antecedents of customer loyalty to the firm. Yet, too many firms continue to pay scant regard to the practice of ethics.

Marketing ethics is the systematic application of moral standards to marketing decisions, behaviours, and institutions (Laczniak and Murphy 1993). This is the application of ethics to the marketing process. Ethics in marketing is not an exact science and the views on what is ethical, and what is not, may vary from person to person or from employer to employee. This is because everyone is driven by a moral compass which may not be compatible with that of another person.

Marketing ethics is an applied discipline, akin to medical ethics, and should be practiced by all marketing functionaries. As such, good ethical practices must be encouraged by the firm as this is a necessary capability required by the firm for coping with the ethical issues that managers are likely to face.

Research has indicated that 65 to 75 percent of all managers will face major ethical dilemmas in their careers (Murphy et al. 2005). These dilemmas may be present when the personal values of the manager are not compatible with the corporate values of the firm and managers are called upon to use moral judgement. This situation can be mitigated by the firm through value statements where the manager working with the firm is obliged to conform to the value system of the firm.

Some of the popular ethical dilemmas faced by managers working in marketing are selling cigarettes to teenagers, selling alcohol to alcoholics, discriminatory pricing for alienating customer segments, ruthless marketing of painkillers, selling substandard products, sex appeal advertising demeaning to women, and hard-selling of goods to compulsive buyers. These scenarios, while not illegal, would hardly meet the desired ethical standards of the socially responsible firm.

Ethical issues in marketing may arise when the customer feels cheated or manipulated by the firm. These issues can be observed with all the elements of the marketing mix. For example, if the product does not meet with the customer's expectations and the customer believes that there was a false claim in the labelling of the product then an ethical issue would arise. So is the case of subliminal advertising that is used by the marketer for getting into the minds of the unsuspecting customer who makes purchases that he or she can ill afford. Ethical issues may also occur with the price of the product where there are hidden charges at the time of the sale and the customer is only made aware of these after the purchase is made. In the case of the place, these ethical issues could arise when a product of a certain standard is distributed in one place while the substandard alternative is distributed in another place.

Buzz Marketing could be viewed as an unethical practice that is carried out by marketers. This often involves the marketing of products through word-of-mouth advertising using opinion leaders, trendsetters, and influencers. These people would market to their followers, often giving the false impression that they are not being paid by the firm and are merely promoting a good product as a free service to the public. The Buzz Marketing technique is popularly used among promoters of alcoholic beverages and particularly effective in marketing to the teenage consumer who are impressionable and quite susceptible to hard sell.

Despite the controversial nature of the marketing practice, social responsibility has become a buzz phrase among industry practitioners. However, the question remains on where does social responsibility start and profit maximization end? The next section will present a brief philosophical discourse on marketing from the utilitarian perspective in an attempt to shed light on this question.

UTILITARIANISM AND MARKETING

The practice of marketing is essentially based on the doctrine of utilitarianism which suggests that an action must be judged based on the greater good or the net benefits accrue to the greater number of people. This doctrine is aimed at producing a moral choice which means that all practical alternatives must be given due consideration and net benefits deduced for each alternative with the selected alternative deemed to have more good than bad consequences. Utilitarianism is also based on the principle of maximizing overall utility, i.e., getting greatest value for the least amount of resources.

This way of operating is demonstrated by marketers in the following scenarios—a pharmaceutical company will market painkillers without highlighting some of the side effects and other consequences from taking the drug. This action may be justified by the marketer on the basis that the millions of people who are benefiting from taking the drug is a greater good than catering to the significantly fewer people that are suffering from its side effects and consequences. And, so, while some may argue that this way of thinking is skewed and not just, this is the popular way of thinking that has emerged with the modern era. Another scenario would be the use of shopping stimulus such as buy one get one to attract impulsive buyers to make unintended purchases. This, again, can be justified on marketing grounds by arguing that the greater good is to provide for the economy segment, which is much larger in numbers, and not to attend to the psychological needs of the impulsive or compulsive, who are fewer in number, and will buy even when they can ill afford to do so.

It is quite understandable and even generally acceptable for business to be carried out on utilitarian grounds as the key objective of the business is to utilize resources based on their utility for maximizing profits. Utilitarian philosophy also entails the assessment of a set of alternative options in a given scenario and selecting the option with best utility. Notably, the utilitarian approach is not in favour of vulnerable groups as they contain the smaller number of people and so the marketing practice is viewed by many as not fair and just. The practice of utilitarianism is engrained in the business school philosophy and has therefore become a part of the operating psyche of the marketing manager.

In the pursuit of ethics and social justice, there are at least two questions to be asked in carrying out the business activity:

1. Who decides on what is the greater good—is it the firm, the market, or the individual?
2. Should generating a net gain for a larger group result in a loss or penalty for the smaller group?

These questions are highly philosophical with answers that will naturally vary across different philosophical schools. And while the answers to these questions are outside the scope of this book, it is believed that the needs and desires of the smaller and disadvantaged groups must be taken into consideration by the marketer, against the backdrop of social and economic justice for all, and despite the necessity of utilitarianism in business.

In this regard and despite the importance of the profit motive, the customer-oriented firm will be well aware that the long-term sustainability of the firm is highly dependent on the trust and commitment between the marketer and the customer. Trust and commitment are desired end states for all firms that seek to protect their reputation in the eyes of the customer. Ethics and social justice should therefore be embraced by the firm as preconditions across all segments, including the compulsive buying, as smaller groups, too, can do harm to the good reputation of the firm. The next section will present a rationale for focusing on the service to compulsive buyers.

SERVING COMPULSIVE BUYERS

Marketing is concerned with the satisfaction of the needs and wants of the customer in a profitable manner. This is done by presenting the offering to the target market at the various touchpoints. In this context, the marketer is faced with the challenge of differentiating between the needs and wants, on the one hand, and the compulsion, on the other. To be socially just and ethically responsible, the marketer has a duty to care for and serve compulsive buyers and those with compulsive buying tendencies. Moreover, these compulsive shoppers provide an income stream that the marketer will want to sustain thus supporting this service on both profitability and ethical grounds. After all, compulsive buyers are heavy spenders on both products and services.

If the compulsive buyer gets too heavily indebted, then he or she will not be able to continue to buy, hence the firm will lose the customer. Needless to say, it is much cheaper to keep an existing customer than to acquire a new one. The marketers must recognize the delicate balance between ethical responsibility and profit sustainability in service to compulsive buyers. This is not dissimilar to the balance struck by the bartender who will not continue to serve a man, on moral grounds, when he is drunk but will once again serve this man, on the grounds of business, when he soberly returns to the bar. In treating with this group, therefore, the marketer must always be mindful of the ethically responsible behaviour that must be employed by the firm. The challenge, therefore, is to develop marketing guidelines that are ethically grounded for addressing the needs and wants of the compulsive buyers. The next section will present a template for identifying compulsive buying tendencies and the full-blown behaviour among shoppers.

Identifying Compulsive Buyers and Tendencies

The marketer must first identify compulsive buyers and their tendencies to effectively serve this vulnerable group. In doing so, the marketer must capture information on consumer traits and utilize this information to determine if a customer is a compulsive buyer or one who has compulsive buying tendencies, i.e., likely to buy compulsively. This information can be captured through customer surveys utilizing the scales in the model presented in chapter 3. The scales for six consumer trait constructs, along with the scale for compulsive buying, are summarized in Table 6.1.

These scale items are measured using five points:

1. strongly disagree
2. disagree
3. neither agree nor disagree
4. agree
5. strongly agree

After the data collection exercise, the data must then be entered and analysed by the marketer to determine the score of each customer on each scale. That is, an index must be developed for each customer on each of the six scales. Where the item in the scale is tagged with an 'R,' i.e., reverse coded, then a score of 1 must be replaced with 5, 2 replaced with 4, 3 remains 3, 4 replaced with 2, and 5 replaced with 1. These indices, computed on their arithmetic means, will range between 1 and 5, and an index that falls between 1 to 3.4 is regarded as a low to medium level of the trait while 3.5 to 5 is considered to be a medium to high level of that trait.

This undertaking has shown that there are four consumer traits that are likely to trigger compulsive buying among shoppers. These are consumer impulsiveness, credit card misuse, vanity, and neurotics (see chapter 3). As such, customers with a medium to high level of any of the four consumer traits should be identified by the marketer as a shopper who is likely to have compulsive buying tendencies—defined here as having sufficient amounts of one or more of the four identified traits. However, if the shopper scores medium to high on the compulsive buying scale itself then that shopper should be identified as a compulsive buyer. This means that the shopper can have the compulsive buying tendencies that trigger the behaviour (scoring medium to high on one or more of the four consumer traits) and not be a full-blown

Table 6.1. Scales and Items of Consumer Traits Constructs and Compulsive Buying

Author(s)	Year	Scale	Items
Roberts & Jones	2001	Credit Card Misuse	• less concerned with price when use card • exceed credit limit • pay off card monthly (R) • impulsive when shop with card • too many cards • worry about card debt • take cash advance on card • spend more with card • make minimum payment • card regularly at maximum credit limit • one card pays another • delinquent on payment
Puri	1996	Consumer Impulsiveness	• impulsive • careless • self-controlled (R) • extravagant • farsighted (R) • responsible (R) • restrained (R) • easily tempted • rational (R) • enjoy spending • planner (R)
Eastman, Goldsmith, & Flynn	1999	Status Consumption	• buy product with status • interest in new product with status • pay more for product with status • product status is irrelevant (R) • place value on snob appeal
Tian, Bearden, & Hunter	2001	Consumer Need for Uniqueness	• collect unusual products/brands to be different • sometimes dared to be different in dressing in ways that others are likely to disapprove • lose interest in product/brand when it becomes popular • break customs and rules in product/brand purchase and situation in which it is used • purchased unusual products/brands to create a more distinctive personal image • purchase one-of-a-kind products/brands to create own style • avoid products/brands that have been accepted and purchased by the average consumer

Author(s)	Year	Scale	Items
Netemeyer, Burton, & Lichtenstein	1995	Vanity	• the look of self is extremely important to person • very concerned with self-appearance • important to always look good • believe people notice how attractive the individual is • believe people are envious of their good looks • believe their body is sexually appealing
Mowen	2000	Emotional Instability	• typically, more moody than others • temperamental (overly emotional) • testy (easily irritated) • emotions go way up and down
Valence, d'Astous & Fortier	1988	Compulsive Buying	• when have money, cannot help but to spend part or all of it • often impulsive in buying behaviour • have an irresistible urge to go into a shop to buy something • often bought product not needed, while knowing very little money left

compulsive buyer (as a compulsive buyer must score medium to high on the compulsive buying scale itself) or could theoretically be a compulsive buyer, though hardly likely, and not possess enough of the traits to trigger a compulsive buying behaviour. Notably, the consumer traits of consumer need for uniqueness and status consumption, while not found to be true predictors of compulsive buying (see chapter 3), must not be ignored by the marketer in the identification process as prior research suggests that these could be drivers in some situations albeit not significant in this undertaking. On this basis therefore, the consumers who score medium to high on consumer need for uniqueness and status consumption should also be flagged as suspected cases of compulsive buying for further assessment.

Marketing to Compulsive Buyers on Ethical Grounds

Marketing ethics is the moral principles and values that guide the operations of the marketing unit. This ethical behaviour is practiced by the socially responsible firm and characterized by transparency, trustworthiness, fairness, integrity, and empathy in dealing with the customers of the firm. Ethical practices will help to promote trust and loyalty to the firm and should not be restricted by firm size. This means that the gamut of firms from small to multinational corporations should be stewards of ethical marketing.

A brand's reputation could be affected in cases where the customer perceives that the firm is not being ethical in its activities. In addition, if the customers associate the brand with excessive consumerism that they believe is leading to problems such as severe personal debts and damaged family relationships then this could negatively affect the way that the customers think of the brand. Importantly, any behaviour that is construed by the customer as unethical could lead to the demise of the brand. This makes the discourse in ethics in marketing quite relevant with the significant role that ethics play in brand health.

Most of the work that links marketing ethics to vulnerable groups have been done in areas such as alcoholism, cigarette smoking, and advertising. However, ethics in marketing is quite novel in the context of service to compulsive buyers as little or no work has been done in this area. This paucity of work continues to exist despite the pervasive nature of compulsive buying and the need for improved understanding of this phenomenon. Besides, marketers play a significant role in facilitating addictive shoppers. This makes the firm an integral partner in the compulsive shopping behaviour of the customer and therefore marketing has an ethical responsibility to help with this problem. Thus, for a company that seeks to improve its brand, the application of marketing ethics and moral standards in service to compulsive buyers is a responsible thing to do and also a path that should be pursued for the sustainable protection of the brand.

The next section will present the ethical considerations in marketing to vulnerable groups that are prone to compulsive buying behaviour and tendencies. It will address the trait groups that are likely to exhibit the behaviour and tendencies—credit card misusers, vanity inclined, impulsive personalities, and the neurotic type personality. It will also discuss the ethics in marketing to demographic groups such as children, teenagers, and women who are also expected to exhibit these compulsive buying behaviours and tendencies. Other ethical considerations for marketing to this vulnerable group will also be discussed. Notably, while ethical considerations are usually discussed in a general sense, an attempt is made in this undertaking to discuss these considerations within each of the vulnerable group categories albeit difficult as some of these considerations may be applied across the categories.

MARKETING ETHICS AND CREDIT CARD MISUSE

The growth in credit card usage has resulted in a large portfolio comparable to the growth in other traditional areas of consumer credit such as bank overdrafts and personal loans (Omar et al. 2014). This makes the credit card a major slice of the risk portfolio of many financial firms. The credit card provides a key source of income for financial firms in annual fees, late fees, cash advance fees, and interest payments from clients who do not pay the full balance on a monthly basis. It also facilitates the spending of cardholders to make purchases that they can ill afford. Marketers have therefore become very aggressive with the lucrative stream of income that can be realized in the credit card business.

Credit card misuse is associated with an excessive and irresponsible spending by the cardholder that often leads to an out-of-control debt (Palan et al. 2011; Sidoti and Devasagayam 2010). The misusers of the card tend to give much less thought to the dollar value of the purchase when using the card as compared to spending with cash (Feinberg 1986; Soman 2001). This misuse of the credit card facility is quite widespread among compulsive buyers who often find themselves with out-of-control debts.

In this undertaking, it was identified that credit card misuse was the number one predictor of compulsive buying (see chapter 3). This finding, therefore, raises ethical concerns in the marketing of credit cards, particularly to the young adult segment where the problem is pervasive. The widespread marketing of credit cards to vulnerable groups was perceived as unethical by the Congress of the United States and led to the enactment of the Credit Card Act 2009 aimed at providing more protection for the affected consumers (see chapter 4). More of these ethical and regulatory considerations need to be initiated by the State for the protection of vulnerable consumers.

The credit card firms should also be mindful that young adults, particularly students, should not be the focus of aggressive credit card marketing as this segment is extremely vulnerable in compulsive buying behaviour (Roberts and Jones 2001). Instead, the banks, for example, should protect these vulnerable youngsters by lowering credit limits, requiring minimum income levels, issuing debit card alternatives, and promoting the hazards (similar to cigarette manufacturers) of credit card usage (Roberts 1998). Consumer education for helping with more judicious usage of credit cards should also be facilitated by these banks. This educational curricular could also include training in personal finance for a more holistic approach to managing money. Some of these interventions are already being done by socially responsible financial institutions. However, more needs to be done in the ethical marketing of credit cards as the misuse of the facility is leading to more financial hardship, more so among compulsive buyers.

Marketing Ethics and the Vanity Inclined

A vanity-predisposed consumer is one who takes excessive pride in one's appearance or accomplishments. This trait is usually associated with physical appearance but may also refer to other things such as accomplishments. To be vain is different from being proud as the former behavioural type is excessive and leads to the unreasonable self-worth or self-importance of the individual. The vanity consumer trait was identified in this undertaking as a key driver of compulsive buying (see chapter 3) and therefore raises an ethical concern for marketing to this vulnerable group—many of whom may not be in a position to pay for the expensive goods that they force themselves to acquire.

In targeting the consumer, advertisers tend to focus on the vanity predisposition of the shopper by creating an aspiration for materialism (e.g., in the purchase of expensive items) while emphasizing that the acquisition will reduce the inner tension in the buyer and make one feel and look attractive (Roberts and Pirog 2004). There is also the issue of vanity sizing, that has become widespread, where brands, particularly clothing companies, deflate label sizes on clothing items (e.g., changing a size 12 label to a size 10) with the principal aim of wanting their customers to feel slim and good about themselves, and, in turn, buy more of the brand. This practice explains why some sizes of clothing items fit in some brands and do not fit in others and thus raises an ethical issue that warrants consideration.

It is no doubt a difficult job to treat the ethical considerations in marketing to the vanity segment. In the case of vanity sizing, we could simply say, albeit not as easy, that clothing manufacturers should refrain from such practice on ethical grounds. However, for treating with the vanity inclined shopper as a whole, the ethical considerations may be complex since vanity connotes a negative perception in the minds of the general population and this group may not be seen as vulnerable, notwithstanding their compulsive buying tendencies. The marketer, too, may not see this group as deserving of special treatment on the count of vanity as after all these are customers who do not appear to have self-esteem issues and are big spenders. That said, and while not being specific to the vanity shopper, the socially responsible firm must always adhere to good ethical standards in treating with all customers.

Marketing Ethics and the Impulsive Personality

An impulsive shopper is one who usually makes a sudden purchase without a plan or without giving much thought to the process (Beatty and Ferrell 1998). Though compulsive buying is qualitatively distinct from impulsive buying (Faber and O'Guinn 2008), compulsive shopping can also be viewed as an extreme case of impulsive buying behaviour with both predispositions leading to excessive and unplanned purchases (Verplanken and Sato 2011). Notably, 75 percent of all purchases are unplanned (Muratore 2016). In this undertaking it was found that the impulsive buying trait among consumers was a key antecedent to compulsive buying (see chapter 3).

This impulsive buying behaviour by the consumer is aided by the marketer as goods bought impulsively account for a significant portion of consumer spending. Retailers, for example, would use sales tactics such as buy one get one using the limited time only tag line to trigger an impulsive purchase. These retailers would also stack their bins en route to the cashier with inexpensive sale items such as candy bars or on-the-go pastry to entice the impulsive shoppers to make unplanned purchases. Retailers, in turn, may argue that the strategic organizing of store items in bins in the proximity of the cashier will also remind the customer of what they need to buy before leaving the store and so this retailing practice does not raise to the level of an ethical concern. This of course is a plausible point of view. It therefore becomes a toss-up on whether marketing is treading on ethical grounds in retail tactics used for selling to impulsive shoppers.

Marketers must, nonetheless, be mindful of their social responsibility to give ethical consideration to all compulsive buyers including those with impulsive tendencies. A good return policy along with store warranty agreements are examples of initiatives that the marketer can take in its service to impulsive buyers. These ethical measures, using taglines such as if you are not 100 percent satisfied then you can return for full purchase price or replace with another item of your choice would at least provide the impulsive shopper with a chance to return the goods at the onset of a post-purchase dissonance. The use of return policies in the retail business model is by no means new and certainly provides a reprieve to all consumers whether or not they are impulsive in the acquisition of goods. However, while these policies may have generalized applicability in service to all consumer groups, they certainly have significant implications for the impulsive buyer who characteristically makes the purchase without giving much thought.

Marketing Ethics and the Emotionally Unstable

The emotionally unstable, otherwise referred to as the neurotic personality type, is one who is moody and often experiences negative feelings manifesting in anxiety, frustration, and anger. These consumers usually find it hard to control their emotions and impulses. It has been suggested that the neurotic personality type shops to satisfy emotional needs and relieve anxiety and consequently shopping goes way beyond the utility of the product for those so inclined. However, shoppers with the neurotic trait tend to display negative consumption-based emotions such as excessive complaining, negative word of mouth, and post-purchase dissonance (Mooradian and Olver 1997). Still, sales promotions are often used by the marketers to target the neurotic personality who is known to buy with the *swing of the mood* and is addictive in buying behaviour. These emotionally unstable buyers are triggered by sales promotions tactics such as the use of coupons, price discounts, samples, and *buy one get one* promos (Gilbert and Jackaria 2002).

In this undertaking, it was determined that the emotionally unstable buyer is likely to exhibit compulsive buying tendencies (see chapter 3). This makes emotional instability an ethical concern in the context of the service provided by the marketer. This also raises questions on what can be done on ethical grounds for treating with this vulnerable group. Again, the answer to this question is not simple since most ethical interventions that can be pursued by the marketer are not specific to any group and are therefore applicable in treating with a wide range of consumer groups. However, in the specific context, albeit applicable to compulsive buyers in general, the marketer could sponsor health and wellness symposiums that are aimed at psycho-social interventions doing sessions in cognitive behaviour therapy, yoga, and meditation. Psycho-social techniques are known to have positive influence on the neurotic personality type. This was demonstrated by Armstrong and Rimes (2016) who found that neurotic personalities were better able to control their emotions using these methods of psychotherapy.

Cognitive behaviour therapy has been described as a *talking* therapy that is used for helping to manage the thoughts, feelings, and emotions of the troubled individual. This approach to psychotherapy is becoming very popular because of its successes in changing the way that people think and behave. Health and wellness professionals who administer these sessions can easily be accessed and the emotionally unstable person can also become proficient at the technique through practice. Similarly, meditation can be quite effective in helping to manage the mood swings of the neurotic type of compulsive buyer. Simply, meditation is a breathing technique with the basic tenets of sitting in a comfortable position, closing the eyes, and breathing deeply. Other fundamentals of meditation include the focusing on the breath, letting go of current thoughts and once again, refocusing on the breath when there are intervening thoughts. These compulsive buyers would then be encouraged to participate in the sessions at no cost as a give back from the firm on socially responsible grounds.

Marketing Ethics and Women

There is long-standing evidence to suggest a disproportionate ratio of females to males who display compulsive buying behaviour with the percentage of females ranging between 74 percent (Hanley and Wilhelm 1992) to over 93 percent (Black et al. 1998). These ratios are quite striking and more recent studies are suggesting that the ratios may not be as disproportionate, but females are still more prevalent in compulsive buying behaviour than males (Weinstein et al. 2016). Moreover, women are believed to make or influence the purchase of more than 80 percent of all products and services sold in the United States (Wharton 2003). Besides, shopping is a major pastime, particularly among women (Black 2007). This makes the woman a significant player in consumer spending and vulnerable to compulsive buying being susceptible to the whims and fancies presented by the marketer. Cosmetics and gifts are two product categories that are associated with impulsive buying among females (O'Guinn and Faber 1989).

A give back to women on ethical grounds was demonstrated by The Body Shop which instead of using the standard chemical ingredients in its products sought out a natural alternative that could be produced in third world countries by poor women and in turn paid these women decent prices for the plants they farm (Stoll 2002). More generally, compulsive buying by females could have significant implications for their children as women play a greater role than men in socializing children on consumption habits. In ameliorating this situation, the socially responsible firm could develop a line item for a child development programme in its marketing budget to provide training in areas such as personal development and financial skills for the children of the vulnerable women.

Marketing Ethics and Children

Children are increasingly becoming victims of advertising campaigns. These children, being underdeveloped in cognitive abilities, do not make well-reasoned decisions in buying products. This group is known to buy on impulse and can easily be reached through shop stimulus and advertising cues. It can, however, be said that children are consumers of goods and services and not customers since the customers are their parents who make the purchases. Marketers are nonetheless aware that children provide a sizable market for goods and services as they are known to influence their parents on product selection and brand choice. Parents, in turn, are losing control in the marketing initiative that is directed at their children. This market for children's goods consists of many product categories such as toys, cereals, and video games and these children are targeted through television advertising and internet sources.

As a vulnerable market segment, these children often cultivate great materialistic orientation leading to conspicuous consumption, compulsive buying, or even shoplifting and later becoming the wrong customer for the firm (Zaharie and Maniu 2012). There have been many reported cases of transgressions in marketing to children. For instance, it has been said that some toys are marketed to young children even when they are considered to be potentially dangerous to their health and safety. These children are unsuspecting and limited in their ability to self-regulate their impulses and therefore become vulnerable to advertising and promotion.

The firm must first do some serious introspection on the ethical implications in marketing to this impressionable group (Zaharie and Maniu 2012). In dealing with the children demographic, the marketer must, at a minimum, ensure they adhere to laws and restrictions governing the marketing activity. Providing shopping education for children in areas such as fast-food consumption would also help to improve buying behaviour. Marketing should also ensure that parents are brought on board when targeting children. For instance, in marketing online games, like Minecraft that is owned by Microsoft, a parent's guide is included to promote child safety, fair play, and the digital wellbeing of the child. Involving the parents in the marketing process should be a mandate of all ethically responsible firms that choose to market to children.

Marketing Ethics and Teenagers

Teenagers, similar to the children demographic, are known to be impulsive purchasers and prone to compulsive buying tendencies. It has been suggested that the tendency to buy compulsively begins in the teenage years (Koran et al. 2006) and becomes reinforced and perpetuated with the passage of time (Richins 2017). d'Atous et al. (1990) found that both parents and peers are influential in driving the compulsive buying tendencies within teenagers. These teens are quite impressionable in their approach to consumption, although you may not be able to convince them that they are, and unplanned consumption is characteristic of this segment. Some of the popular product categories that are marketed to this target group include movies, cigarettes, alcohol, video games, and soft drinks.

Ethical considerations must be given in marketing to this vulnerable group of compulsive buyers. At a minimum, buyer beware standards must be promoted by the marketers. This would include advertising of movie ratings (e.g., adults only and X-rated), highlighting consequences of cigarette smoking, providing restrictions for alcohol consumption, providing cautioning instructions for playing video games, and messaging the health risk associated with sugary drink consumption. The promoting of the buyer beware standards is already being done in some industries but needs to be more widespread across industries.

GENERALIZED ETHICAL CONSIDERATIONS FOR MARKETING TO COMPULSIVE BUYERS

Ethical considerations are usually generalized across groups and not specific to vulnerable groups. These generalized guidelines are, nonetheless, applicable to marketing in the context of compulsive buyers. In this regard, Murphy et al. (2005) identified several maxims that could aid the marketer when faced with an ethical issue.

- The golden rule—act in the way you would like others to act towards you.
- The professional rule—do what you think is proper in the eyes of your professional colleagues.
- The TV/Newspaper test—ask yourself if you would feel comfortable explaining the marketing action on TV or on the front page of a newspaper to the general public.
- When in doubt, don't—if you feel uneasy about a decision, then that is reason enough to question it.
- Slippery slope—don't start something now, knowing that it will lead to failure in the future.
- Kid/mother/founder on your shoulder—would your child, mother, or company founder be comfortable with your ethical decision.
- Silver rule—never knowingly do harm.

These guiding principles, if adopted, should help with the ethical issues that may be faced by the marketers and will also be of good value to the wider practice of marketing. In addition to these ethical maxims, Murphy et al. (2005) highlighted six ethical values that were developed by the American Marketing Association for providing further ethical guidance to marketers.

1. Honesty—the marketer must be truthful and forthright in all dealings with customers and stakeholders.
2. Responsible—the marketer must accept the consequences of the marketing decisions and strategies.
3. Fairness—the marketer must seek to balance the needs of the buyer with the interest of the seller.
4. Respect—the marketer must give regard to the basic human dignity of all stakeholders.
5. Openness—the marketer must be transparent in all marketing activities and operations.
6. Citizenship—the marketer must fulfil economic, philanthropic, legal, and societal responsibilities in service to stakeholders.

These maxims and ethical values have general applicability and can also be adopted across other functional areas. The socially responsible firm has a duty to the customer and the society at large and should therefore use these guiding principles as a template for developing their own value systems.

In the final analysis, the marketer should reflect on modifications that could be made to the marketing programme with a view to preventing compulsive buyers from spending on items that they cannot afford (Mikolajczak-Degrauwe and Brengman 2014). In addition, these marketers could assist the compulsive buyers by sponsoring a *Shop Responsible* campaign that will serve as a vehicle for stimulating the customer to evaluate the purchasing motive and assess the risk before making the purchase (Horváth and Birgelen 2015). These initiatives would aid customer satisfaction and could bolster customer loyalty to the firm.

Ethical Readiness for Treating with Compulsive Buyers

A delicate balance must be struck between ethical marketing and persuasive marketing of goods and services. This is necessary for the long-term sustainability of the firm as customer loyalty in the long run will require equity and fairness between customer and firm. Ethical marketing on the one hand suggests that the marketer must be exemplary in conduct, being truthful and fair in the offering provided to the customers. Persuasive marketing on the other hand suggests that the marketer must always seek to influence the customer to buy with the view of maximizing the profitability of the firm.

In its treatment of compulsive buyers, the firm must pursue and maintain a programme of ethical readiness adopted to its marketing behaviour and actions. Readiness for marketing to compulsive buyers must be assessed on five dimensions namely, social responsibility, reputation, equity and fairness, action, and evaluation. The programme of readiness must utilize guided questions that are to be answered by the firm. These questions are summarized as follows.

1. Social Responsibility
   a. To what extent do we have a social and societal obligations to compulsive buyers?
   b. How do we square with our social and societal duties to other vulnerable groups?
2. Reputation
   a. How does the duty to compulsive buyers synchronize with our organization's values?
   b. What will our customers say about us?

    c. Are the personal values of managers aligned with the value systems of the firm?

3. Equity and Fairness
   a. Do we practice good ethics in service to all stakeholders?
   b. How far do we go with the doctrine of utilitarianism?
   c. Are we fair in our marketing to compulsive buyers?
   d. How do we benefit in providing ethical service to compulsive buyers?
   e. Will we lose money if we ramp-up the ethical service provided to compulsive buyers?
   f. How do we strike a balance in power between the compulsive buyer and the marketer?
   g. Do we provide a good return to our shareholders?

4. Action
   a. How do we identify compulsive buyers?
   b. What ethical services should we provide to compulsive buyers?
   c. Do we have a code of ethical conduct for marketing?
   d. How do we create an ethicist or ethical champion within the firm?

5. Evaluation
   a. What results will make us satisfied?
   b. How does ethical practice impact return on investment?
   c. Are marketing actions and decisions ethically validated?

The ethical code of conduct for marketing to compulsive buyers should then be informed by the answers to these questions.

CLOSING COMMENTS

Marketing management has the fiduciary responsibility to provide shareholders with a fair return on investment on capital. This utilitarian maxim of doing business could create ethical issues in the mind of the marketer as generating wealth for the shareholder may not be in congruence with the needs and aspirations of the consumer. Moreover, compulsive buying is a reality that is faced by many customers and even those customers who would not normally be characterized as compulsive may buy compulsively as this can be triggered by impulsiveness, vanity seeking, neuroticism, and credit card misuse. This extended group therefore is not expected to be too small. As such, to address the needs of this vulnerable group, it may be socially responsible to provide supporting services for the troubled individuals at the expense of a greater good such as maximizing customer value of the loyalty segment or maximizing shareholder wealth.

The issue of protecting consumers from compulsive type shopping is also a responsibility of the State, and many countries have legal regulations in place for controlling sale and use of products such as tobacco, alcohol and gambling. Compulsive behaviours, if not self-regulated, may have severe social and psychological consequences for the consumer. Verplanken and Sato (2011) noted that while many State regulations may not protect the consumer from impulsive buying behaviour, many countries are utilizing Sales of Goods Acts to provide consumer protection thus allowing the buyer to return the goods that were purchased impulsively if they were not regarded as satisfactory or fit for the purpose described by the seller. Under these circumstances, the buyer would be entitled to a full refund. Nonetheless, shopping compulsion is the ultimate responsibility of the consumer and the shopper must guard against this behaviour through the practice of self-regulation. Information should also be provided to these consumers by both State and firm for mitigating their compulsivity.

The decision to extend support to compulsive buyers, in all likelihood, may be seen as going against the grain of utility and would hardly get the support of some managers. On the other hand, servicing the needs of the compulsive buyer may also be viewed as a long-term strategy that could pay dividends in the future as compulsive buyers are big spenders, and would be expected to be loyal with the support provided by the firm. It therefore becomes a matter of social responsibility and an aspirational decision to serve compulsive buyers on ethical grounds. In the final analysis, ethics will require good judgement that will come from the personal characteristics, experience, and training of the manager, and should be entrenched as a guiding principle of marketing management.

More research is, however, needed to measure the perceived or actual vulnerability and subsequent susceptibility of compulsive buyers to marketing programmes (Gupta 2013). This could be carried out with the aid of contemporary techniques such as neuromarketing for a deeper understanding of the nuanced issue of relating marketing ethics to compulsive buying (Stanton et al. 2017). Such work, if properly executed and its findings effectively disseminated, could help to convince the marketing community of the need for serious interventions in this area.

Conclusion

SIZE-UP

This conclusion commences with a brief size-up of the book project and presents the lessons learnt from the study on compulsive buying behaviour. Addictive shopping is a widespread problem which results in a large number of shoppers having an uncontrollable and obsessive urge to buy excessively. The individual with this disposition is likely to have insecurity issues, low self-esteem, and mood problems. Many of these shoppers have problems with their family and professional lives that are attributed to this compulsive behaviour.

The marketer's job is to woo the customer into satisfying consumer needs and desires by buying. Many customers will buy even when the items are not needed and they can ill afford to do so. At the same time, shopping might be discouraged through societal influence, which includes family and friends, and, therefore, it is not uncommon to hear negative shopping stereotypes such as we shop too much or the buyer must beware. Nonetheless, shopping is a necessary activity whether or not we shop perfunctorily or compulsively.

The shopping situation creates a conundrum for the compulsive buyer as this individual will shop to assuage depressive feelings while simultaneously engaging in the negative thoughts about shopping. This makes compulsive buying a complex cognitive problem for the shopper who is being challenged to manage both mind and money. That said, compulsive buying is an integrative problem that is linked to both the consumer traits and the self-regulatory processes. The marketers, who benefit from this vulnerability, have a social responsibility to give ethical consideration in the services provided to this group. In this project, we sought to develop an integrative framework for relating consumer traits and self-regulation to compulsive shopping behaviour and also addressed the ethical considerations in marketing to this vulnerable group.

Some of the previous research in this area presented compulsive buying behaviour as a mental health disorder that resembles conditions such as obsessive-compulsive disorder, impulse control disorder, mood disorder, and addictive disorder while others likened this shopping behaviour to a shopping-stimulus-response problem that resembles impulsive buying. This latter view is one that is often expressed in the marketing literature. Moreover, there is no consensus on the categorization of compulsive buying in the mental health literature and perhaps this could be a reason why the disorder was not listed in the latest edition, i.e., the 5th edition, of *The American Psychiatric Association's Diagnostic and Statistical Manual of Mental Disorders* (DSM-5) and was also not listed in the World Health Organization's (WHO) international classification of diseases (Harnish, Bridges, and Karelitz 2017).

Compulsive buying has also been compared with other dysfunctional behavioural types such as alcoholism and gambling where common grounds are found in the addictive nature of these problems. Our position is that compulsive buying has features of both a mental health disorder and a stimulus-response shopping problem. This, we believe, is a reasonable and pragmatic position to take based on our review of the existing literature.

The cause of compulsive buying is still in doubt (Black 1996) and there is certainly no single reason that can be attributed to this behaviour (Faber and O'Guinn 2008). However, there is evidence to suggest that compulsive buying is associated with consumer traits (DeSarbo and Edwards 1996). This would include traits such as emotional instability and impulsiveness. Consumer traits are characteristics of individual differences applied to the consumer and are represented by consistent patterns of consumption, thoughts, feelings and behaviours (Joachimsthaler and Lastovicka 1984). These traits are mere subsets of the basic personality traits. However, there is no general classification of what constitutes a consumer trait except that the trait is associated with consumer consumption. Compulsive buying itself is viewed as a consumer trait and classified by Mowen (2000) as a surface or higher order trait, representing an enduring disposition for product category and consumption.

Mowen (2000) advanced that personality traits are arranged in a hierarchy in which elemental traits, at the base of the hierarchy, are linked to compound traits, which in turn are linked to situational traits and, ultimately, to surface traits which stand at the top of the trait hierarchy. These traits appear to be more tangible the higher you get in the hierarchy between elemental traits and surface traits. Notably, the higher order trait of compulsive buying is demonstrated as behaviours such as excessive and unwanted buying that are characteristic of compulsive buyers and may easily be observed in the shopper's actions despite the complex nature of these behaviours.

Mowen (2000) suggested that lower level traits are useful in predicting and explaining higher order traits, although traits at one level may be helpful in predicting traits at the same or at higher levels. It may not always be easy to identify the level of the consumer trait. However, researchers try to predict higher order traits that are more easily observed. Further, based on the prior research that seeks to associate consumer traits with compulsive buying, it was theorized by the authors of this book that the higher order trait of compulsive buying could be predicted by six traits that were prevalent among consumers. These assumptions were used to build the predictive model, highlighted in chapter 3, that consisted of the consumer traits of consumer impulsiveness, status consumption, consumer need for uniqueness, credit card misuse, vanity, and emotional instability, all mapped to the surface trait of compulsive buying. The findings from the model tested revealed that four of these consumer traits were successful in predicting the compulsive buying behaviour of the shopper. These are impulsiveness, vanity disposition, emotional instability, and credit card misuse.

Credit card misuse was found to be the strongest predictor of compulsive buying from the model presented in the project. Notably, this misuse of the credit card is also considered to be trait-like as there is an enduring pattern of this behaviour in that shoppers who are misusers of the credit card tend to do so with some consistency and not merely incidentally. Not surprisingly, therefore, credit card misuse provides a conduit to compulsive buying as this facility allows the consumer to make the purchase from future income, thus temporarily ignoring the pain of paying, and also encourages the shopper to spend more than he or she would spend when shopping with cash.

Self-regulation has been identified as a necessary process for addressing the compulsive buying problem. This is a process by which one monitors and manages one's inner state and behaviours towards the attainment of positive goals and outcomes. Self-regulation is an internal control that is essential for regulating human behaviour and is akin to a muscle; and like the muscle, and through practice, this internal mechanism can be bolstered for better performance and outcomes. The process of self-regulation must be activated by the consumer for better choices (Baumeister 2018). Indeed, the mechanism of self-control has significant implications for the compulsive buyer, thus making the study of self-regulating compulsive buying behaviour still relevant, given the pervasive nature of the shopping problem. Notwithstanding the obvious importance for a better understanding of the link between self-regulation and compulsive buying, the existing literature has uncovered mere semblance of work in this area and so in chapter 5 of this project an attempt was made to explicate this association using an epistemological approach and a conceptual model drawn from the current knowledge. Strategies were also presented for self-regulating compulsive buying behaviour with highlights on the consumer traits, identified in chapter 3, that were key drivers of this addictive behaviour.

Marketing ethics is the systematic application of moral standards to marketing decisions, behaviours, and institutions (Laczniak and Murphy 1993). Similar to the case of self-regulating compulsive buying behaviour, there is little or no evidence of work in the existing literature on ethical considerations in marketing to this vulnerable group. Mind you, the extant literature speaks to marketing ethics vis-à-vis women and children shoppers (groups with compulsive buying tendencies) but the discussions have been a mere semblance on ethical considerations in marketing to compulsive buyers. This gap was therefore filled by this project through the discussions that ensued in chapter 6. No doubt, the practice of marketing raises the ethical question on whether marketing is designed to exploit the vulnerability of customers through their physical and psychological needs. These marketers generated the shopping urge through advertising, promotion, and shopping stimuli and consequently the compulsive shopper will get out of control with spending to satisfy that euphoric feeling associated with shopping. In defence of marketing, the socially responsible firm pursues ethical practices as a give back to its customers.

There are seven key lessons that were learnt from the study of compulsive buying behaviour.

1. People who are likely to buy compulsively can reasonably be identified from a set of related consumer traits.
2. The consumer traits of consumer impulsiveness, credit card misuse, vanity and emotional instability are key drivers of compulsive buying behaviour.
3. Credit card misuse is the number one driver of compulsive buying behaviour.
4. The average shopper has low levels of the traits of impulsiveness, credit card misuse, emotional instability, and compulsive buying and moderate levels of the vanity trait.
5. Shoppers with compulsive buying tendencies are likely to buy compulsively and fully fledged compulsive buyers will engage in addictive shopping even when they do not have the consumer trait tendencies.
6. Compulsive buying behaviour can be controlled by consumers through a process of self-regulation.
7. There are ethical considerations in marketing to compulsive buyers.

LESSONS LEARNT

This section will provide a brief discussion on each of the seven lessons.

Lesson 1: People Who Are Likely to Buy Compulsively Can Reasonably Be Identified from a Set of Related Consumer Traits

Compulsive buying itself is a trait-like disposition that can be classified as a surface or higher-order consumer trait. Mowen (2000), through the development of the 3M model, concluded that some consumer traits were associated with other trait types and that lower-order traits such as neuroticism were effective in predicting higher order and more tangible trait types such as compulsive buying.

The review of the existing literature revealed that many consumer traits were associated with compulsive buying. These include:

1. emotional instability
2. consumer impulsiveness
3. extraversion
4. status consumption
5. consumer need for uniqueness
6. credit card misuse
7. vanity
8. materialism
9. openness to new experience
10. self-esteem
11. conscientiousness
12. agreeableness

Some of these traits were not included in the reduced model discussed in chapter 3 as the intra trait analysis revealed that many of the traits had underlying items that were either similar or highly correlated across traits, a condition referred to as multicollinearity in the psychology literature, and so these confounding traits were dropped in search for a predictive model that reflected both parsimony and robustness.

A reduced model of six independent consumer traits was therefore developed for predicting and explaining the outcome trait of compulsive buying. This model demonstrated that four of the six consumer traits were significant predictors of compulsive buying and 40 percent of this addictive behaviour was attributed to the six traits. These results we found to be quite substantial since as few as six traits were responsible for explaining so much of compulsive buying behaviour when most studies in consumer behaviour explain no more that 20 percent of the dependent outcome (Hair et al. 2014). The model was therefore deemed to be robust, and it was concluded that people who are likely to buy compulsively (i.e., the output variable in the model) can be identified from a set of related consumer traits (i.e., the set of predictor traits). Moreover, there is compelling evidence to suggest that personality traits account for more explanation of consumer behaviour, such as compulsive buying, than consumer researchers tend to recognise (Mowen 2000). For this reason, the other traits identified through the review of the literature but were not included in the model in chapter 3, should not be ignored as they, too, are potential predictors of compulsive buying albeit not empirically tested in this undertaking.

Lesson 2: The Consumer Traits of Consumer Impulsiveness, Vanity, Emotional Instability, and Credit Card Misuse are Key Drivers of Compulsive Buying

The model developed in chapter 3 identified consumer impulsiveness, credit card misuse, vanity and emotional instability as significant and positive predictors of compulsive buying. Thus, the shopper who has any of these trait dispositions is likely to buy compulsively. Moreover, with this positive association, it means that shoppers in whom these consumer traits are more pronounced will likely be more addictive in buying behaviour than those in whom those traits are less distinctive.

Impulsive buying resembles compulsive buying behaviour (Verplanken and Sato 2011) and so it was not surprising when we found that consumer impulsiveness was strongly associated with compulsive buying. This impulsiveness is generally triggered by external shopping stimuli thus causing a bit of uneasiness in the mind of the shopper that leads to the purchase. The impulsive shopper may also develop an internal feeling of anxiety or a depressive mood and, in turn, buys compulsively to alleviate this feeling.

The vanity inclined will generally focus on appearance. These shoppers tend to be materialistic and fashion conscious. Fashion interests are often compulsive in buying behaviour (Park and Burns 2005) with an internal drive to keep up their appearance. The vanity personality is known to spend on high-end brands often to impress others. It therefore appears that the more we think about impressing others, the more likely will we develop the urge to buy compulsively.

There is a long stream of research that has associated emotional instability or the neurotic personality type with compulsive buying (Andreassen et al.

2013; Mikolajczak-Degrauwe et al. 2012; Thompson and Prendergast 2015). Consistent with expectations therefore, this undertaking has revealed similar results. The neurotic personality type is believed to buy compulsively to mitigate that depressive feeling that is associated with emotional instability. And so, in the mind of the person who has the neurotic disposition, making the purchase will generate a sense of relief, even for short periods, thus escaping the low feeling that often besets this personality type.

It has been suggested that the aggressive marketing of the credit card is responsible for the high levels of compulsive buying among college students (Benson et al. 2010). Credit card marketing has also induced compulsive buying among other demographics. Moreover, the misuse of the card, particularly when the shopper has multiple credit cards, is positively associated with compulsive buying (Roberts 1998). As expected therefore, the use of multiple credit cards could prove difficult for the shopaholic to manage and so this facility is easily misused. Further, credit card misuse was found to be a strong predictor of the compulsive purchase of clothing among women (Sari and Suyasa 2017).

Lesson 3: Credit Card Misuse Is the Number One Driver of Compulsive Buying Behaviour

The present study found that credit card misuse was the strongest predictor of compulsive buying in the model developed in chapter 3. Whether compulsive buying is viewed as a mental health disorder or a shopping stimulus-response behaviour (and it is perhaps a little of both), the credit card provides a conduit to buying compulsively as it helps addictive shoppers to temper their anxieties, knowing well that with the card they can more easily make the purchase than they could with cash, thus mitigating the pain of paying since paying takes place at a later date after the tendering of the card.

The credit card also facilitates the euphoric feeling of buyer's high, i.e., the intense excitement that the compulsive buyer experiences while shopping, since without the card the buyer would likely be more apprehensive about the purchase. Moreover, the buyer may not be clear on whether he or she can afford the goods, and so this excitement that comes with buying compulsively would be stifled if one did not have the wherewithal to tender the credit card.

Lesson 4: The Average Shopper Has Low Levels of the Traits of Impulsiveness, Credit Card Misuse, Emotional Instability, and Compulsive Buying, and Moderate Levels of the Vanity Trait

One of the distinct advantages in working with consumer traits is that the level of the trait possessed by the individual can reasonably be measured with numbers using standard psychometric scales (Browne and Kaldenberg 1997). These numbers can be utilized in further computations for producing both descriptive and inferential insights on these traits. In addition, there are two schools of thought on personality traits with the first suggesting that all consumers have all shopping-related traits to a lesser or greater extent and the second indicating that some consumers have some traits to varying degrees but do not have other traits. This undertaking adopted the first school of thought and in the assessment of addictive shopping behaviour all customers in the sample were asked to self-report on each of the traits including compulsive buying on scales ranging from a low of 1 to a high of 5. See Table C.1 for descriptive statistics on the traits that were significantly related to compulsive buying.

Table C.1. Descriptive Statistics on Consumer Traits

	Impulsiveness	Credit Card Misuse	Vanity	Emotional Instability	Compulsive Buying
N	175	175	175	175	175
Mean	2.3569	1.9681	3.3619	2.3971	1.9029
Median	2.3636	1.9167	3.3333	2.5000	1.7500
Mode	2.55	1.33	2.67	1.00	1.00
Std. Deviation	.65989	.61033	.81207	1.03813	.84918
Minimum	1.00	1.00	1.00	1.00	1.00
Maximum	5.00	5.00	5.00	5.00	5.00

Most shoppers do not see themselves as emotionally unstable or compulsive buyers judging from the modal values presented in the table. Similarly, shoppers, on average, reported low levels of impulsiveness, credit card misuse, emotional instability and moderate levels of the vanity disposition judging from the central tendency statistics in general. Notably, these traits are triggers of compulsive buying behaviour and low levels of the trait will not cause addictive buying as the low-level traits are associated with low levels of compulsive buying based on the positive association. Conversely, high levels of these traits would be associated with high levels of the addictive behaviour. It may, therefore, be a good estimate that compulsive buyers are represented by a prevalence rate varying from 1 percent to 8 percent in the general population (Weinstein et al. 2016). Gladly, the majority of shoppers have low levels of these traits that are causal to compulsive buying.

Lesson 5: Shoppers with Compulsive Buying Tendencies Are Likely to Buy Compulsively and Full-Fledged Compulsive Buyers Will Engage in Addictive Shopping Even When They Do Not Have the Consumer Trait Tendencies

The significant positive association between each of the four consumer traits (consumer impulsiveness, vanity, emotional instability, and credit card mis-use) and compulsive buying (that was found from this undertaking) suggests that shoppers who have medium to high levels of any of these traits would be more likely to buy compulsively than those possessing low levels of the traits. Notably, a medium to high level of any of these traits is indicative of a compulsive buying tendency of the shopper. Similarly, a shopper who has a medium to high level of the compulsive buying trait itself is deemed to be a compulsive buyer. See chapter 6 on identifying compulsive buyers and tendencies.

These compulsive buying tendencies that are identified by the medium to high levels of the four consumer traits will trigger the compulsive buying be-haviour among the shoppers. However, a full-fledged compulsive buyer will seemingly engage in addictive shopping even when that person does not have any of the four trait tendencies for triggering compulsive buying behaviour. It is very unlikely though that full fledge compulsive buyers will not have compulsive buying tendencies that are depicted by these predictor traits.

Lesson 6: Compulsive Buying Behaviour Can Be Controlled by Consumers through a Process of Self-Regulation

The shopper is faced with external forces (e.g., marketing stimuli and macro forces) and internal forces (e.g., moods, feelings, emotions, attitudes and consumer traits) in the everyday course of shopping. Too many shoppers are challenged to manage these forces and succumb to compulsive buying behaviour. The shopper must self-regulate to mitigate this buying behaviour. To offer an approach to self-regulation, the book draws on the Regulatory Focus Theory (Higgins 1998) and Self Regulation Theory (Baumeister and Vohs 2007b).

The Regulatory Focus Theory suggests that the compulsive buyer could be predisposed to either a promotion orientation or a prevention orientation in pursuit of the purchase (Higgins 1998). Promotion focused means that the buyer is motivated by growth and development needs while prevention fo-cused means that the buyer is motivated by security needs and avoiding losses (Brockner and Higgins 2001).

The Self Regulation Theory suggests that the compulsive buyer is predis-posed to a feedback loop of setting standards, developing the motivation and willpower to meet these standards, and monitoring the compulsive buying behaviour for attaining the desired results (Baumeister and Vohs 2007b).

The shopaholic must go through a cognitive process when faced with a shopping situation. First, the compulsive buyer should get a handle on his or her buying orientation (promotion/prevention) and then align the thoughts of self-regulation with the buying orientation. Second, the buyer should take into consideration the buying cues and forces, along with those as-sociated predispositions such as vanity and impulsiveness and consciously self-regulate the buying behaviour despite these forces. Third, this buying situation should be processed through the feedback loop of setting standards and developing motivation and willpower while monitoring for achieving the desired outcome. Taking it all together, the self-regulatory process is com-plex. However this is the kind of reasoning that the compulsive buyer must go through for controlling the habit.

Lesson 7: There Are Ethical Considerations in Marketing to Compulsive Buyers

Compulsive buyers are no doubt a vulnerable market segment and marketers have an ethical responsibility to provide extra service to this troubled group. After all, compulsive buyers and shoppers with these tendencies are major contributors to the firm's revenues and so the marketer's responsibility is both ethical and fiduciary given the significant financial implications. On ethical grounds, the marketer should first identify these addictive shoppers then develop the ethical readiness of the firm for dealing with the segment and ultimately provide support for the addictive shoppers through interven-tion strategies and programmes.

The ethical considerations in marketing to shoppers with compulsive buy-ing behaviour should be focused on consumers with compulsive buying traits (credit card misusers, the vanity inclined, impulsive personalities, and the neurotic type personality) and on vulnerable segments such as women, chil-dren, and teenagers who are prone to compulsive buying tendencies. Some of these ethical considerations are summarized next.

- Banks should protect vulnerable young people by lowering credit limits, requiring minimum income levels, issuing debit card alternatives and pro-moting the hazards (similar to cigarette manufacturers) of credit card us-age (Roberts 1998). Notably, much of this is already being done, but more needs to be done and be more widespread and entrenched.
- Clothing manufacturers should refrain from the practice of vanity sizing that has become widespread, where brands, particularly clothing compa-

nies, deflate label sizes on clothing items (e.g., changing a size 12 label to a size 10) with the principal aim of wanting their customers to feel slim, and good about themselves, and, in turn, buy more of the brand.

- Taglines such as "if you are not 100 percent satisfied then you can return for full purchase price or replace with another item of your choice" would at least provide the impulsive shopper with a chance to return the goods at the onset of a post purchase dissonance.
- Marketers should sponsor health and wellness programmes that are aimed at psycho-social interventions doing sessions in cognitive behaviour therapy, yoga, and meditation. Psycho-social techniques are known to have a positive influence on the impulsive and neurotic personality type.
- The firm could develop a line item for a child development programme in its marketing budget to provide training in areas such as personal development and financial skills for the children of the vulnerable women.
- In dealing with the children demographic, the marketer must, at a minimum, ensure they adhere to laws and restrictions that govern the marketing activity.
- Buyer beware standards must be promoted by the marketers particularly for the benefit of vulnerable groups.

CLOSING COMMENTS

This book has addressed the pervasive problem of compulsive buying utilizing an integrative approach that includes consumer traits, self-regulation, and marketing ethics. The conceptualization of the manuscript was in response to the authors' view that a combined approach was needed to address the multilayered problem of compulsive buying behaviour. Moreover, the large majority of literature on compulsive buying is presented through the academic articles and so it was felt that a detailed and integrative discourse was required for more insightful coverage on the subject. It was decided that a book would be needed to provide this treatment since only a few books were found in this area and these did not go far enough to address the drivers and solutions of addictive shopping. This book on compulsive buying was therefore written with focus on the troika of consumer personality, self-regulation, and marketing ethics—three areas that are central to addictive shopping habits.

The use of consumer traits in the predictive model has paid dividends in this project as the traits provided a significant portion of the explanation (40 percent for buying compulsively. The internal process of self-regulation was found to be a force for mitigating this buying behaviour. As such, the skill of self-regulation must be honed by the compulsive buyer and the various techniques of self-control, such as cognitive behaviour therapy, yoga, and meditation, should be practiced by the shopper for helping with this problem.

In a bid to mitigate compulsive buying behaviour, the shopper must be mindful that the shopping process is a dialogue of self and soul and a search for external reflections of the internal being (Benson 2000). Looking internally is a first step in dealing with this addictive problem. This mind game must be managed by the shopper for the customer to buy judiciously in these times of heightened consumerism. The marketer, in turn, must be sensitive to the ethical considerations in dealing with this vulnerable group notwithstanding the much needed profit motivation of the modern firm. Twinning of the marketing activity with the act of being ethically responsible is certainly a very important strategy for sustaining the firm.

One of the distinctive features of this book is that the problem of compulsive buying is addressed from the angles of both the buyer and the seller. Of note is that the seller's side is presented through the ethical considerations in marketing to this group. The book should therefore be of benefit to both the individual and the firm. Students, graduate and undergraduate, who are pursuing their programme of study in business schools and in the social and behavioural sciences should find the work useful. The book is targeted at an international audience and is not intended to be country specific in its discourse.

Another important feature of the work is that the manuscript was written in easily understood language, utilizing simple examples and scenarios to be consumed by a wide cross-section of readers yet grounded in scholarship, to benefit academics, as it utilizes theories and other epistemological underpinnings of the scholarly discourse. The general public should also find interest in this book as it advances an understanding of the role of consumer traits in compulsive buying behaviour and the self-regulation of this behaviour towards better buying habits.

The seven lessons learnt in this undertaking serve as a major part of the contribution of this work. The lessons are related and the empirical model for predicting compulsive buying was central in uncovering these lessons. It is hoped that the book will shed light and deepen the understanding of compulsive buying behaviour.

Taken together, the book presented an integrated framework of the compulsive buying process with strategies for self-regulation and ethical considerations for marketing goods and services to compulsive buyers. The work commenced with a discourse on the compulsive buying process and transitioned to the role of consumer traits in addictive shopping behaviour. A model for predicting compulsive buying behaviour was next presented along with a discourse on credit card misuse—found to be the number one driver of compulsive buying. The discussion on the credit card was followed up with a conceptual model for self-regulating compulsive buying behaviour and the integrated framework was concluded with detailed discussion on the ethical considerations for marketing to the troubled buyers. The book concludes with the lessons learnt from this undertaking and brief comments that highlight the intended beneficiaries of the work.

References

Achtziger, Anja, Marco Hubert, Peter Kenning, Gerhard Raab, and Lucia Reisch. 2015. "Debt Out of Control: The Links between Self-Control, Compulsive Buying, and Real Debts." *Journal of Economic Psychology* 49: 141–49.

Adamczyk, Grzegorz, Jorge Capetillo-Ponce, and Dominik Szczygielski. 2020. "Compulsive Buying in Poland: An Empirical Study of People Married or in a Stable Relationship." *Journal of Consumer Policy* 43, no. 4: 1–18.

Ahmed, Naveed, Omer Farooq, Junaid Iqbal, Bahaudin Zakariya, and Mohammad Ali. 2014. "The Relationship among Vanity Trait, Shopping Values and Compulsive Buying: An Evidence from University Shoppers." *European Journal of Business and Management* 6, no. 28: 160–70.

Allport, Gordon W., and Henry S. Odbert. 1936. "Trait-Names: A Psycho-Lexical Study." *Psychological Monographs* 47, no. 1: i–171.

Allport, Gordon Willard. 1968. *The Person in Psychology*. Boston: Beacon Press.

Andreassen, Cecilie Schou, Mark D. *Griffiths*, Siri Renate *Gjertsen*, Elfrid *Krossbakken*, Siri *Kvam*, and Ståle *Pallesen*. 2013. "The Relationships between Behavioural Addictions and the Five-Factor Model of Personality." *Journal of Behavioral Addictions* 2, no. 2: 90–99.

Andreassen, Mark D. *Griffiths*, Siri Renate *Gjertsen*, Elfrid *Krossbakken*, Siri *Kvam*, and Ståle *Pallesen*. 2013. "Impulsivity: Integrating Cognitive, Behavioral, Biological and Environmental Data." In McCown, William G., Judith L. Johnson, and Myrna B. Shure. (Eds.), *The Impulsive Client: Theory, Research, and Treatment*. Washington, DC: American Psychology Association, 39–56.

Ariely, Dan, and Jeff Kreisler. 2017. *Dollars and Sense: How We Misthink Money and How to Spend Smarter*. New York: HarperCollins.

Armstrong, Lauren, and Katharine A. Rimes. 2016. "Mindfulness-Based Cognitive Therapy for Neuroticism (Stress Vulnerability): A Pilot Randomized Study." *Behavior Therapy* 47, no. 3: 287–98.

Ashton, Michael C., and Kibeom Lee. 2009. "The HEXACO-6: A Short Measure of the Major Dimensions of Personality." *Journal of Personality Assessment* 91, no. 4: 340–45.

Awanis, Sandra, and Charles Chi Cui. 2014. "Consumer Susceptibility to Credit Card Misuse and Indebtedness." *Asia Pacific Journal of Marketing and Logistics* 26, no. 3: 408–29.

Babin, Barry J., and William R. Darden. 1995. "Consumer Self-Regulation in a Retail Environment." *Journal of Retailing* 71, no. 1: 47–70.

Bandura, Albert. 1989. "Social Cognitive Theory." In Vasta, Ross (Ed.), *Annals of Child Development*. vol. 6. *Six Theories of Child Development* (pp. 1–60). Greenwich, CT: JAI Press.

Bandura, Albert. 1991. "Social Cognitive Theory of Self-Regulation." *Organizational Behavior and Human Decision Processes* 50, no. 2: 248–87.

Barelds, Dick P. H. 2005. "Self and Partner Personality in Intimate Relationships." *European Journal of Personality* 19: 501–18.

Barratt, Ernest S. 1993. "Impulsivity: Integrating Cognitive, Behavioral, Biological, and Environmental Data." In McCown, W. G., J. L. Johnson, & M. B. Shure (Eds.), *The impulsive client: Theory, research, and treatment* (pp. 39–56). Washington, DC: American Psychological Association.

Baumeister, Roy F. 1990. "Suicide as Escape from Self." *Psychological Review* 97, no. 1: 90–113.

Baumeister, Roy F. 2002. "Yielding to Temptation: Self-Control Failure, Impulsive Purchasing, and Consumer Behavior." *Journal of Consumer Research* 28, no. 4: 670–76.

Baumeister, Roy F. 2014. "Self-Regulation, Ego Depletion, and Inhibition." *Neuropsychologia* 65: 313–19.

Baumeister, Roy F. and Kathleen D. Vohs. 2018. "Strength Model of Self-Regulation as Limited Resource: Assessment, Controversies, Update." In *Self-Regulation and Self-Control: Selected works of Roy F. Baumeister* (pp. 78–128). London: Routledge.

Baumeister, Roy F., and Kathleen D. Vohs. 2007a. *Encyclopedia of Social Psychology*. Thousand Oaks, CA: Sage.

Baumeister, Roy F., and Kathleen D. Vohs. 2007b. "Self-Regulation, Ego Depletion, and Motivation." *Social and Personality Psychology Compass* 1, no. 1: 115–28.

Baumeister, Roy F., and Kathleen D. Vohs. 2016. "Strength Model of Self-Regulation as Limited Resource: Assessment, Controversies, Update." In *Advances in Experimental Social Psychology* 54: 67–127.

Baumeister, Roy F., Matthew Gailliot, C. Nathan DeWall, and Megan Oaten. 2006. "Self-Regulation and Personality: How Interventions Increase Regulatory Success, and How Depletion Moderates the Effects of Traits on Behavior." *Journal of Personality* 74, no. 6: 1773–1802.

Baumeister, Roy F., and Todd F. Heatherton. 1996. "Self-Regulation Failure: An Overview." *Psychological Inquiry* 7, no. 1: 1–15.

Baumeister, Roy F., Todd F. Heatherton, and Diane M. Tice. 1994. *Losing Control: How and Why People Fail at Self-Regulation*. Cambridge, MA: Academic Press.

Beatty, Sharon E., and M. Elizabeth Ferrell. 1998. "Impulse Buying: Modelling Its Precursors." *Journal of Retailing* 74, no. 2: 169–91.

Benson, April Lane (Ed.). 2000. *I Shop, Therefore I Am: Compulsive Buying and the Search for Self*. Lanham, MD: Jason Aronson.

Benson, April Lane, Helga Dittmar, and R. Wolfsohn. 2010. "Compulsive Buying: Cultural Contributors and Consequences." In Aboujaoude, Elias, and Lorrin M. Koran (Eds.), *Impulse Control Disorders*. New York: Cambridge University Press, 23–33.

Benson, April L., and David A. Eisenach, 2013. "Stopping Overshopping: An Approach to the Treatment of Compulsive-Buying Disorder." *Journal of Groups in Addiction & Recovery* 8: 3–2

Benson, April Lane, and Marie Gengler. 2004. "Treating Compulsive Buying." In Holman Coombs, Robert (Ed.), *Handbook of Addictive Disorders: A Practical Guide to Diagnosis and Treatment*. Hoboken, NJ: Wiley.

Bighiu, Georgiana, Adriana Manolică, and Cristina Teodora Roman. 2015. "Compulsive Buying Behavior on the Internet." *Procedia Economics and Finance* 20: 72–79.

Black, Claudia. 2012. "Addictive Disorders: The Legacy of Family Trauma." *Psychology Today*. Retrieved 20 November 2020, from https://www.psychologytoday. com/us/blog/the-many-faces-addiction/201209/addictive-disorders.

Black, Donald W. 1996. "Compulsive Buying: A Review." *Journal of Clinical Psychiatry* 57 (suppl. 8): 50–55.

Black, Donald W. 2007. "A Review of Compulsive Buying Disorder." *World Psychiatry* 6: 14–18.

Black, Donald W., Susan Repertinger, Gary R. Gaffney, and Janelle Gabel. 1998. "Family History and Psychiatric Comorbidity in Persons with Compulsive Buying." *American Journal of Psychiatry* 155: 960–63.

Bourke, Rosamund, Leslie J. Francis, and Mandy Robbins. 2004. "Locating Cattell's Personality Factors within Eysenck's Dimensional Model of Personality: A Study among Adolescents." *North American Journal of Psychology* 6, no. 1: 167–74.

Brazier, Yvette. 2018. "What Is Psychology and What Does It Involve?" *Medical News Today*. Retrieved 23 October 2020, from https://www.medicalnewstoday. com/articles/154874.

Brockner, Joel, and E. Tory Higgins. 2001. "Regulatory Focus Theory: Implications for the Study of Emotions at Work." *Organizational Behavior and Human Decision Processes* 86, no. 1: 35–66.

Brockner, Joel, E. Tory Higgins, and Murray B. Low. 2004. "Regulatory Focus Theory and the Entrepreneurial Process." *Journal of Business Venturing* 19, no. 2: 203–20.

Browne, Beverly A., and Dennis O. Kaldenberg. 1997. "Conceptualizing Self-Monitoring: Links to Materialism and Product Involvement." *Journal of Consumer Marketing* 14, no. 1: 31–44.

Bryan, Bob. 2015. "Credit Card Companies Have Sent Out 3.2 Billion Pieces of Mail This Year, and That's Not Even Close to the Record." *BusinessInsider.com*. Retrieved 18 October 2020, from http://www.businessinsider.com/credit-card-companies-32-billion-pieces-of-mail-this-year-2015–11.

Bryant, Peter. 2009. "Self-regulation and Moral Awareness among Entrepreneurs." *Journal of Business Venturing* 24, no. 5: 505–18.

Burton, Dawn. 2012. *Credit and Consumer Society*. London: Routledge.

Cakarnis, Jakob, and Steve Peter D'Alessandro. 2015. "Does Knowing Overcome Wanting? The Impact of Consumer Knowledge and Materialism Upon Credit Card Selection with Young Consumers." *Young Consumers* 16, no. 1: 50–70.

Cattell, Raymond B., and John R. Nesselroade. 1967. "Likeness and Completeness Theories Examined by Sixteen Personality Factor Measures on Stably and Unstably Married Couples." *Journal of Personality and Social Psychology* 7, no. 4: 351–61.

Cherry, Kendra. 2017. "Main Branches of Psychology. Explore Psychology." Retrieved 23 October 2020, from https://www.explorepsychology.com/branches-of-psychology.

Chinomona, Richard. 2013. "An Empirical Examination of the Predictors of Consumer Compulsive Buying as an 'Impulse Control Disorder Not Otherwise Specified': A Branding Perspective." *Journal of Applied Business Research* 29, no. 6: 1689–1704.

Claes, Laurence, Patricia Bijttebier, Frederique Van Den Eynde, James E. Mitchell, Ron Faber, Martina de Zwaan, and Astrid Mueller. 2010. "Emotional Reactivity and Self-Regulation in Relation to Compulsive Buying." *Personality and Individual Differences* 4, no. 5: 526–530.

Coombs, Robert Holman. 2004. *Handbook of Addictive Disorders: A Practical Guide to Diagnosis and Treatment*. Hoboken, NJ: Wiley.

Christenson, Gary A., Ronald J. Faber, Martina De Zwaan, Nancy C. Raymond, Sheila M. Specker, Michael D. Ekern, Thomas B. Mackenzie, Ross D. Crosby, Scott J. Crow, and Elke D. Eckert. 1994. "Compulsive Buying: Descriptive Characteristics and Psychiatric Comorbidity." *Journal of Clinical Psychiatry* 55, no. 1: 5–11.

Csikszentmihalyi, Mihaly, and Eugene Rochberg-Halton. 1981. *The Meaning of Things: Domestic Symbols and the Self*. New York: Cambridge University Press.

Dammeyer, Jesper. 2020. "An Explorative Study of the Individual Differences Associated with Consumer Stockpiling during the Early Stages of the 2020 Coronavirus Outbreak in Europe." *Personality and Individual Differences* 167: 110263. Retrieved 15 September 2021, from https://doi.org/10.1016/j.paid.2020.110263.

Darrat, Aadel A., Mahmoud A. Darrat, and Douglas Amyx. 2016. "How Impulse Buying Influences Compulsive Buying: The Central Role of Consumer Anxiety and Escapism." *Journal of Retailing and Consumer Services* 31: 103–8.

d'Astous, Alain. 1990. "An Inquiry into the Compulsive Side of Normal Consumers." *Journal of Consumer Policy* 13: 15–31.

Davenport, Thomas H. 2006. "Competing on Analytics." *Harvard Business Review* (January): 1–10.

de Paula, Jonas J. de, Danielle de S. Costa, Flavianne Oliveira, Joana O. Alves, Lídia R. Passos, and Leandro F. Malloy-Diniz. 2015. "Impulsivity and Compulsive Buying Are Associated in a Non-Clinical Sample: An Evidence for the Compulsivity-Impulsivity Continuum?" *Brazilian Journal of Psychiatry* 37, no. 3: 242–44.

Dera, Gabriella. 2018. "Three Marketing Strategies to Boost Credit Card ROI." *The Financial Brand*, 26 October 2018. Retrieved 5 January 2021, from https://thefinancialbrand.com/75905/credit-card-marketing-strategies-bank-credit-union-roi/.

DeRubeis, Robert J., Daniel R. Strunk, and Lorenzo Lorenzo-Luaces. 2016. "Mood Disorders." In Norcross, John C., Gary R. VandenBos, and Donald K. Freedheim (Eds.), *APA Handbook of Clinical Psychology: Psychopathology and Health* 4 (pp. 31–59). Retrieved 15 September 2021, from https://doi.org/10.1037/14862-002.

DeSarbo, Wayne S., and Elizabeth A. Edwards. 1996. "Typologies of Compulsive Buying Behaviour: A Constrained Clusterwise Regression Approach." *Journal of Consumer Psychology* 5, no. 3: 231–62.

Digman, John M. 1990. "Personality Structure: Emergence of the Five-Factor Model." *Annual Review of Psychology* 41: 417–40.

Dittmar, Helga. 2004. "Understanding and Diagnosing Compulsive Buying." In Holman *Coombs, Robert (Ed.), Handbook of Addictive Disorders: A Practical Guide to Diagnosis and Treatment*. Hoboken, NJ: Wiley.

Dittmar, Helga. 2005. "Compulsive Buying: A Growing Concern? An Examination of Gender, Age, and Endorsement of Materialistic Values as Predictors." *British Journal of Psychology* 96, no. 4: 467–91.

Dittmar, Helga, Karen Long, and Rod Bond. 2007. "When a Better Self Is Only a Button Click Away: Associations between Materialistic Values, Emotional and Identity–Related Buying Motives, and Compulsive Buying Tendency Online." *Journal of Social and Clinical Psychology* 2, no. 3: 334–61.

Donnelly, Grant, Masha Ksendzova, and Ryan T. Howell. 2013. "Sadness, Identity, and Plastic in Over-Shopping: The Interplay of Materialism, Poor Credit Management, and Emotional Buying Motives in Predicting Compulsive Buying." *Journal of Economic Psychology* 39: 113–25.

Duhachek, Adam, and Dawn Iacobucci. 2005. "Consumer Personality and Coping: Testing Rival Theories of Process." *Journal of Consumer Psychology* 15, no. 1: 52–63.

Eastman, Jacqueline K., Ronald E. Goldsmith, and Leisa Reinecke Flynn. 1999. "Status Consumption in Consumer Behavior: Scale Development and Validation." *Journal of Marketing Theory and Practice* 7, no. 3: 41–52.

Eisenberg, Ian W., Patrick G. Bissett, A. Zeynep Enkavi, Jamie Li, David P. MacKinnon, Lisa A. Marsch, and Russell A. Poldrack. 2019. "Uncovering the Structure of Self-Regulation through Data-Driven Ontology Discovery." *Nature Communications* 10, no. 2319.

Elliott, Richard. 1994. "Addictive Consumption: Function and Fragmentation in Postmodernity." *Journal of Consumer Policy* 17, no. 2: 159–79.

Ellis, Albert, Mike Abrams, and Lidia Abrams. 2008. *Personality Theories: Critical Perspectives*. Thousand Oaks, CA: Sage.

Ercis, Aysel, and Musa Unalan. 2017. "Relationship among Big Five Personality Traits, Compulsive Buying and Variety Seeking." *Journal of Management Marketing and Logistics* 4, no. 3: 217–23.

Eysenck, Hans J. 1951. "The Organization of Personality." *Journal of Personality* 20, no. 1: 101–17.

Faber, Ronald J. 2004. "Self-Control and Compulsive Buying." In Kasser, T., and A. D. Kanner (Eds.), *Psychology and Consumer Culture: The Struggle for a Good Life in a Materialistic World* (pp. 169–187). Washington, DC: American Psychological Association. Retrieved 26 October 2020, from https://doi.org/10.1037/10658–010.

Faber, Ronald J., and Gary A. Christenson. 1996. "In the Mood to Buy: Differences in the Mood States Experienced by Compulsive Buyers and Other Consumers." *Psychology and Marketing* 13, no. 8: 803–19.

Faber, Ronald J., and Thomas C. O'Guinn. 1992. "A Clinical Screener for Compulsive Buying." *Journal of Consumer Research* 19, no. 3: 459–69.

Faber, Ronald J., and Thomas. C. O'Guinn. 2008. "Compulsive Buying: Review and Reflection." In Haugtvedt, Curtis P., Paul M. Herr, and Frank R. Kardes (Eds.). *Handbook of Consumer Psychology*. London: Taylor & Francis.

Fang, Xiang, and John C. Mowen. 2009. "Examining the Trait and Functional Motive Antecedents of Four Gambling Activities: Slot Machines, Skilled Card Games, Sports Betting, and Promotional Games." *Journal of Consumer Marketing* 26, no. 2: 121–31.

Fauth-Bühler, Mira, Karl Mann, and Marc N. Potenza. 2016. "Pathological Gambling: A Review of the Neurobiological Evidence Relevant for Its Classification as an Addictive Disorder." *Society for the Study of Addiction* 22: 885–97.

Feinberg, Richard A. 1986. "Credit Cards as Spending Facilitating Stimuli: A Conditioning Interpretation." *Journal of Consumer Research* 13: 348–56.

Fenton-O'Creevy, Mark, Sally Dibb, and Adrian Furnham. 2018. "Antecedents and Consequences of Chronic Impulsive Buying: Can Impulsive Buying Be Understood as Dysfunctional Self-Regulation?" *Psychology & Marketing* 35, no. 3: 175–88.

Forgas, Joseph P., Roy F. Baumeister, and Dianne M. Tice. 2009. "The Psychology of Self-Regulation: An Introductory Review." *Psychology of Self-Regulation: Cognitive, Affective, and Motivational Processes* 11: 1–17.

Freeman, Andrea. 2013. "Payback: A Structural Analysis of the Credit Card Problem." *Arizona Law Review* 55: 151–99.

Gensler, Sonja, Peter C. Verhoef, and Martin Böhm. 2012. "Understanding Consumers' Multichannel Choices across the Different Stages of the Buying Process." *Marketing Letters* 23, no. 4: 987–1003.

Gilbert, D. C., and N. Jackaria. 2002. "The Efficacy of Sales Promotions in UK Supermarkets: A Consumer View." *International Journal of Retail & Distribution Management* 30, no. 6: 315–22.

Gohary, Ali, and Kambiz Heidarzadeh Hanzaee. 2014. "Personality Traits as Predictors of Shopping Motivations and Behaviors: A Canonical Correlation Analysis." *Arab Economic and Business Journal* 9, no. 2: 166–74.

Goldsmith, Ronald E., Leisa Reinecke Flynn, and Elizabeth B. Goldsmith. 2015. "Consumer Characteristics Associated with Compulsive Buying." *Journal of Multidisciplinary Research* 7, no. 3: 21–38.

Goldsmith, Toby., and Susan L. McElroy. 2000. "Compulsive Buying: Diagnosis, Associated Disorders and Drug Treatment." In Benson, A. L. (Ed.), *I Shop, Therefore I Am: Compulsive Buying and the Search for Self* (pp. 217–42). Lanham, MD: Jason Aronson.

Goleman, Daniel. 1991. "A Constant Urge to Buy: Battling a Compulsion. *New York Times*, 18 July 1991. Retrieved 22 July 2019, from https://www.nytimes.com/1991/07/17/garden/a-constant-urge-to-buy-battling-a-compulsion.html.

Gollwitzer, Peter M., and Paschal Sheeran. 2009. "Self-Regulation of Consumer Decision Making and Behavior: The Role of Implementation Intentions." *Journal of Consumer Psychology* 19, no. 4: 593–607.

Granero, Roser, Fernando Fernández-Aranda, Trevor Steward, Gemma Mestre-Bach, Marta Baño, Amparo del Pino-Gutiérrez, Laura Moragas et al. 2016. "Compulsive Buying Behavior: Characteristics of Comorbidity with Gambling Disorder." *Frontiers in Psychology* 7: 625.

Grant, Jon E. 2003. "Three cases of Compulsive Buying Treated with Naltrexone." *International Journal of Psychiatry in Clinical Practice* 7: 223–25.

Grant, Jon E., Brian Odlaug, and Sun Won Kim. 2013. "Impulse Control Disorders: Clinical Characteristics and Pharmacological Management." *Psychiatric Times*. Retrieved 15 September 2020, from https://www.psychiatrictimes.com/view/impulse-control-disorders-clinical-characteristics-and-pharmacological-management.

Gregory, Christina. 2020. "Mood Disorders: General Background Information on Mood Disorders." *Psycom*. Retrieved 15 October 2020, from https://www.psycom.net/mood-disorders/.

Gupta, Rina, and Jeffrey L. Derevensky. 1998. "An Empirical Examination of Jacob's General Theory of Addictions: Do Adolescent Gamblers Fit the Theory?" *Journal of Gambling Studies* 14, no. 1: 17–49.

Gupta, Shruti. 2013. "A Literature Review of Compulsive Buying—A Marketing Perspective." *Journal of Applied Business and Economics* 14, no. 1: 43–48.

Hagedorn, W. Bryce. 2009. "The Call for a New Diagnostic and Statistical Manual of Mental Disorders Diagnosis: Addictive Disorders." *Journal of Addictions & Offender Counselling* 29: 110–27.

Hagedorn, W. Bryce, and Holly J. Hartwig Moorhead. 2010. "The God-Shaped Hole: Addictive Disorders and the Search for Perfection." *Counselling and Values* 55: 63–78.

Hair, Joseph F., G. Tomas M. Hult, Christian M. Ringle, and Marko Sarstedt. 2014. *A Primer on Partial Least Squares Structural Equation Modeling (PLS-SEM)*. Thousand Oaks, CA: Sage.

Hair, Joseph F., Christian M. Ringle, and Marko Sarstedt. 2011. "PLS-SEM: Indeed a Silver Bullet." *Journal of Marketing Theory and Practice* 19: 139–51.

Hanley, Alice, and Mari S. Wilhelm. 1992. "Compulsive Buying: An Exploration into Self-esteem and Money Attitudes." *Journal of Economic Psychology* 13: 5–18.

Harnish, Richard J., K. Robert Bridges, and Joshua L. Karelitz. 2017. "Compulsive Buying: Prevalence, Irrational Beliefs and Purchasing." *International Journal of Mental Health Addiction* 15: 993–1007.

Hayward, Laura C., and Meredith E. Coles. 2009. "Elucidating the Relation of Hoarding to Obsessive Compulsive Disorder and Impulse Control Disorders." *Journal of Psychopathology and Behavioural Assessment* 31: 220–27.

He, Heping, Monika Kukar-Kinney, and Nancy M. Ridgway. 2018. "Compulsive Buying in China: Measurement, Prevalence, and Online Drivers." *Journal of Business Research* 91: 28–39.

Heshmat, Shahram. 2018. "5 Patterns of Compulsive Buying: How Do You Know You Have an Addiction?" *Psychology Today*. Retrieved 20 November 2020, from https://www.psychologytoday.com/us/blog/science-choice/201806/5-patterns-compulsive-buying.

Higgins, E. Tory. 1998. "Promotion and Prevention: Regulatory Focus as a Motivational Principle." *Advances in Experimental Social Psychology* 30: 1–46.

Higgins, E. Tory. 2002. "How Self-Regulation Creates Distinct Values: The Case of Promotion and Prevention Decision Making." *Journal of Consumer Psychology* 12, no. 3: 177–91.

Higgins, E. Tory. 2012. "Regulatory Focus Theory." In Van Lange, Paul A. M., Arie W. Kruglanski, and E. Tory Higgins (Eds.), *Handbook of Theories of Social Psychology* (pp. 483–504). Thousand Oaks, CA: Sage. Retrieved 22 July 2020, from https://doi.org/10.4135/9781446249215.n24.

Hirschman, Elizabeth C. 1979. "Differences in Consumer Purchase Behavior by Credit Card Payment System." *Journal of Consumer Research* 6, no. 1: 58–66.

Hirschman, Elizabeth C. 1992. "The Consciousness of Addiction: Toward a General Theory of Compulsive Consumption." *Journal of Consumer Research* 19: 155–79.

Hoch, Stephen J., and George F. Loewenstein. 1991. "Time-Inconsistent Preferences and Consumer Self-Control." *Journal of Consumer Research* 17, no. 4: 492–507.

Horváth, Csilla, and Marcel Van Birgelen. 2015. "The Role of Brands in the Behavior and Purchase Decisions of Compulsive Versus Noncompulsive Buyers." *European Journal of Marketing* 49, no. 1/2: 2–21.

Jacobs, Durand F. 1989. "Illegal and Undocumented: A Review of Teenage Gambling and the Plight of Children of Problem Gamblers in America." In Schaffer, Howard J., Sharon A. Stein, Blasé Gambino, and Thomas N. Cummings (Eds.), *Compulsive Gambling: Theory, Research and Practice*. Lanham, MD: Lexington Books/D.C. Heath and Company.

Japutra, Arnold, Yuksel Ekinci, and Lyndon Simkin. 2019. "Self-Congruence, Brand Attachment and Compulsive Buying." *Journal of Business Research* 99: 456–63.

Joachimsthaler, Erich A., and John L. Lastovicka. 1984. "Optimal Stimulation Level: Exploratory Behavior Models." *Journal of Consumer Research* 11, no. 3: 830–35.

Job, Veronika, Carol S. Dweck, and Gregory M. Walton. 2010. "Ego Depletion—Is It All in Your Head? Implicit Theories About Willpower Affect Self-Regulation." *Psychological science* 21, no. 11: 1686–93.

John, O. P., Angleitner, A., and F. Ostendorf. 1988. "The Lexical Approach to Personality: A Historical Review of Trait Taxonomic Research." *European Journal of Personality* 2: 171–203.

Johnson, Kim K. P., and Jongeun Rhee. 2008. "An Investigation of Consumer Traits and Their Relationship to Merchandise Borrowing with Undergraduates." *Journal of Family & Consumer Sciences Education* 26: 1–13.

Joireman, Jeff, Jeremy Kees, and David Sprott. 2010. "Concern with Immediate Consequences Magnifies the Impact of Compulsive Buying Tendencies on College Students' Credit Card Debt." *Journal of Consumer Affairs* 44, no. 1: 155–78.

Kara, Ali, Erdener Kaynak, and Orsay Kucukemiroglu. 1996. "An Empirical Investigation of US Credit Card Users: Card Choice and Usage Behavior." *International Business Review* 5, no. 2: 209–30.

Kasser, Tim Ed, and Allen D. Kanner (Eds.). 2004. *Psychology and Consumer Culture: The Struggle for a Good Life in a Materialistic World.* Washington, DC: American Psychological Association.

Kellett, Stephen, and Jessica V. Bolton. 2009. "Compulsive Buying: A Cognitive—Behavioural Model." *Clinical Psychology and Psychotherapy* 16: 83–99.

Kesebir, Sermin, Sema İşitmez, and Duru Gündoğar. 2012. "Compulsive Buying in Bipolar Disorder: Is it a Comorbidity or a Complication?" *Journal of Affective Disorders* 136, no. 3: 797–802.

Khare, Arpita. 2013. "Credit Card Use and Compulsive Buying Behaviour." *Journal of Global Marketing* 26: 28–40.

Kiesel, Meghan. 2012. "Secrets and Scandals of First Ladies: The Secrets and Scandals of Generations of First Ladies." ABC News. Retrieved 20 October 2020, from https://abcnews.go.com/Politics/OTUS/secrets-scandals-ladies/story?id=16652913.

Kingston, Drew A. 2015. "Debating the Conceptualization of Sex as an Addictive Disorder." *Current Addiction Reports* 2, no. 3: 195–201.

Koran, Lorrin M., Kim D. Bullock, Heidi J. Hartston, and Vincent D'Andrea. 2002. "Citalopram Treatment of Compulsive Shopping: An Open-label Study." *The Journal of Clinical Psychiatry* 63, no. 8: 704–8.

Koran, Lorrin M., Ronald J. Faber, Elias Aboujaoude, Michael D. Large, and Richard T. Serpe. 2006. "Estimated Prevalence of Compulsive Buying Behavior in the United States." *American Journal of Psychiatry* 163, no. 10: 1806–12.

Kunst, Jennifer. 2014. "What Is Psychoanalysis? Breaking the Stereotypes and Revealing the Facts about Psychoanalysis." *Psychology Today.* Retrieved 23 October 2020, from https://www.psychologytoday.com/us/blog/headshrinkers-guide-the-galaxy/201401/what-is-psychoanalysis.

Kuzma, John M., and Donald W. Black. 2006. "Compulsive Shopping: When Spending Begins to Consume the Consumer." *Current Psychiatry* 5, no. 7: 27–40.

Laczniak, Eugene R., and Patrick E. Murphy. 1993. *Ethical Marketing Decisions: The Higher Road.* Hoboken, NJ: Prentice Hall.

Lades, Leonhard K. 2014. "Impulsive Consumption and Reflexive Thought: Nudging Ethical Consumer Behavior." *Journal of Economic Psychology* 41: 114–28.

LaRose, Robert. 2001. "On the Negative Effects of E-Commerce: A Sociocognitive Exploration of Unregulated On-Line Buying." *Journal of Computer-Mediated Communication* 6, no. 3: JCMC631.

LaRose, Robert, and Matthew S. Eastin. 2002. "Is Online Buying Out of Control? Electronic Commerce and Consumer Self-Regulation." *Journal of Broadcasting & Electronic Media* 46, no. 4: 549–64.

Lastovicka, John L. 1982. "On the Validation of Lifestyle Traits: A Review and Illustration." *Journal of Marketing Research* 19, no. 1: 126–38.

Laursen, Brett, Lea Pulkkinen, and Ryan Adams. 2002. "The Antecedents and Correlates of Agreeableness in Adulthood." *Developmental Psychology* 38, no. 4: 591–603.

Lea, Stephen E. G., Paul Webley, and Catherine M. Walker. 1995. "Psychological Factors in Consumer Debt: Money Management, Economic Socialization, and Credit Use." *Journal of Economic Psychology* 16, no. 4: 681–701.

Lejoyeux, Michel, and Aviv Weinstein. 2010. "Compulsive Buying." *American Journal of Drug and Alcohol Abuse* 36: 248–53.

Li, Wei, Xuemei Wu, Yayun Sun, and Quanju Zhang. 2010. "Credit Card Customer Segmentation and Target Marketing Based on Data Mining." In *2010 International Conference on Computational Intelligence and Security* (December): 73–76. IEEE.

Limbu, Yam B. 2017. "Credit Card Knowledge, Social Motivation, and Credit Card Misuse among College Students." *International Journal of Bank Marketing* 35, no. 5: 842–65.

Lo, Hui-Yi, and Nigel Harvey. 2011. "Shopping without Pain: Compulsive Buying and the Effects of Credit Card Availability in Europe and the Far East." *Journal of Economic Psychology* 32, 1: 79–92.

Maccarrone-Eaglen, Agata, and Peter Schofield. 2017. "Compulsive Buying Behavior: Re-evaluating ils Dimensions and Screening." *Journal of Consumer Behaviour* 16, no. 5: 463–73.

Magee, Allison. 1994. "Compulsive Buying Tendency as a Predictor of Attitudes and Perceptions." *Advances in Consumer Research* 21: 590–94.

Mann, Ronald J. 2006. *Charging Ahead: The Growth and Regulation of Payment Card Markets*. Cambridge: Cambridge University Press.

Manning, Robert D. 2000. *Credit Card Nation: The Consequences of America's Addiction to Credit*. New York: Basic Books.

Mavri, Maria, and George Ioannou. 2004. "An Empirical Study for Credit Card Approvals in the Greek Banking Sector." *Operational Research* 4, no. 1: 29.

McCrae, Robert R., and Paul T. Costa Jr. 1999. "A Five Factor Theory of Personality." In Pervin, Lawrence A., and Oliver P. John (Eds.), *Handbook of Personality: Theory and Research* (2nd ed.). New York: Guilford.

McCrae, Robert R., and Paul T. Jr. 2004. "The NEO–PI–3: A More Readable Revised NEO." *Journal of Personality Assessment* 84, no. 3: 261–70.

McElroy, Susan L., Paul E. Keck, Harrison G. Pope, Jacqueline M. R. Smith, and Stephen M. Strakowski. 1994. "Compulsive Buying: A Report of 20 Cases." *Journal of Clinical Psychiatry* 55: 242–48.

Mestel, Rosie. 1994. "Drug Brings Relief to Big Spenders." *New Scientist* (November 12): 7.

Mikołajczak-Degrauwe, Kalina, and Malaika Brengman. 2014. "The Influence of Advertising on Compulsive Buying—The Role of Persuasion Knowledge." *Journal of Behavioral Addictions* 3, no. 1: 65–73.

Mikołajczak-Degrauwe, Kalina, Malaika Brengman, Gina Rossi, and Birgit Wauters. 2012. *Does Personality Affect Compulsive Buying? An Application of the Big Five Personality Model*. INTECH Open Access Publisher.

Mischel, Walter. 1996. "From Good Intentions to Willpower." In Gollwitzer, Peter M., and John A. Bargh (Eds.), *The Psychology of Action* (pp. 197–218). New York: Guilford.

Mithaug, Dennis E. 1993. *Self-Regulation Theory: How Optimal Adjustment Maximizes Gain*. Westport, CT: Praeger Publishers/Greenwood Publishing Group.

Mooradian, Todd A., and James M. Olver. 1997. "'I Can't Get No Satisfaction': The Impact of Personality and Emotion on Postpurchase Processes." *Psychology & Marketing* 14, no. 4: 379–93.

Mowen, John C. 2000. *The 3M Model of Motivation and Personality: Theory and Empirical Applications to Consumer Behaviour*. Boston: Kluwer Academics.

Mowen, John C., and Nancy Spears. 1999. "Understanding Compulsive Buying among College Students: A Hierarchical Approach." *Journal of Consumer Psychology* 8, no. 4: 407–30.

Mueller, Astrid, Laurence Claes, James E. Mitchell, Steve A. Wonderlich, Ross D. Crosby, and Martina De Zwaan. 2010. "Personality Prototypes in Individuals with Compulsive Buying Based on the Big Five Model." *Behaviour Research and Therapy* 48, no. 9: 930–35.

Müller, Astrid, Matthias Brand, Laurence Claes, Zsolt Demetrovics, Martina De Zwaan, Fernando Fernández-Aranda, Randy O. Frost et al. 2019. "Buying-Shopping Disorder—Is There Enough Evidence to Support Its Inclusion in ICD-11?" *CNS Spectrums*: 1–6.

Muratore, Isabelle. 2016. "Teens as Impulsive Buyers: What Is the Role of Price?" *International Journal of Retail & Distribution Management* 44, no. 11: 1166–80.

Muraven, Mark, and Roy F. Baumeister, 2000. "Self-Regulation and Depletion of Limited Resources: Does Self-Control Resemble a Muscle?" *Psychological Bulletin* 126: 247–59.

Muraven, Mark, Roy F. Baumeister, and Dianne M. Tice. 1999. "Longitudinal Improvement of Self-regulation through Practice: Building Self-Control Strength through Repeated Exercise." *Journal of Social Psychology* 139, no. 4: 446–57.

Muraven, Mark, and Elisaveta Slessareva. 2003. "Mechanisms of Self-Control Failure: Motivation and Limited Resources." *Personality and Social Psychology Bulletin* 29, no. 7: 894–906.

Murphy, Patrick E., Gene R. Laczniak, Norman E. Bowie, and Thomas A. Klein. 2005. *Ethical Marketing*. Upper Saddle River, NJ: Pearson.

Myers, David G. 2000. "The Funds, Friends, and Faith of Happy People." *American Psychologist* 55: 56–67.

Nataraajan, Rajan, and Brent G. Goff. 1992. "Manifestations of Compulsiveness in the Consumer-Marketplace Domain." *Psychology & Marketing* 9, no. 1: 31–44.

Netemeyer, Richard G., Scot Burton, and Donald R. Lichtenstein. 1995. "Trait Aspects of Vanity: Measurement and Relevance to Consumer Behavior." *Journal of Consumer Research* 2, no. 4: 612–26.

Nichols, Hannah. 2018. "What Is Obsessive-Compulsive Disorder?" Medical News Today. Retrieved 16 October 2020, from https://www.medicalnewstoday.com/articles/178508.php.

Nicoli de Mattos, Cristiana, Hyoun S. Kim, Marinalva G. Requião, Renata F. Marasaldi, Tatiana Z. Filomensky, David C. Hodgins, and Hermano Tavares. 2016. "Gender Differences in Compulsive Buying Disorder: Assessment of Demographic and Psychiatric Co-morbidities." *PLoS ONE*: 11.

Norvilitis, Jill M., Michelle M. Merwin, Timothy M. Osberg, Patricia V. Roehling, Paul Young, and Michele M. Kamas. 2006. "Personality factors, money attitudes, financial knowledge, and credit-card debt in college students 1." *Journal of Applied Social Psychology* 36, no. 6: 1395–13.

Norum, Pamela S. 2008. "The role of Time Preference and Credit Card Usage in Compulsive Buying Behaviour." *International Journal of Consumer Studies* 32, no. 3: 269–75.

Oaten, Megan, and Ken Cheng. 2007. "Improvements in Self-control from Financial Monitoring." *Journal of Economic Psychology* 28, no. 4: 487–501.

O'Guinn, Thomas C., and Ronald J. Faber. 1989. "Compulsive Buying: A Phenomenological Exploration." *Journal of Consumer Research* 16, no. 2: 147–57.

Omar, Nor Asiah, Ruzita Abdul Rahim, Che Aniza Che Wel, and Syed Shah Alam. 2014. "Compulsive Buying and Credit Card Misuse among Credit Card Holders: The Roles of Self-Esteem, Materialism, Impulsive Buying and Budget Constraint." *Intangible Capital* 10, no. 1: 52–74.

Otero-López, José Manuel, and Estíbaliz Villardefrancos. 2013. "Five-Factor Model Personality Traits, Materialism, and Excessive Buying: A Mediational Analysis." *Personality and Individual Differences* 54, no. 6: 767–72.

Palan, Kay M., Paula C. Morrow, Allan Trapp, and Virginia Blackburn. 2011. "Compulsive Buying Behavior in College Students: The Mediating Role of Credit Card Misuse." *Journal of Marketing Theory and Practice* 19, no. 1: 81–96.

Papadimitriou, Odysseas. 2012. "5 Strategies Every Credit Card Marketing Exec Should Implement." *The Financial Brand*, 16 March. Retrieved 5 January 2021, from https://thefinancialbrand.com/22799/5-credit-card-marketing-strategies/.

Parekh, Ranna. 2017. "What Are Bipolar Disorders?" American Psychiatric Association. Retrieved from https://www.psychiatry.org/patients-families/bipolar-disorders/what-are-bipolar-disorders.

Park, Hye-Jung. 2003. "Compulsive Buying of Fashion Goods Purchasers on TV Home Shopping Shows." *Journal of the Korean Society of Clothing and Textiles* 27, no. 5: 588–99.

Park, Hye-Jung, and Leslie Davis Burns, 2005. "Fashion Orientation, Credit Card Use, and Compulsive Buying." *Journal of Consumer Marketing* 22, no. 3: 135–41.

Paunonen, Sampo V. 1998. "Hierarchical Organization of Personality and Prediction of Behaviour." *Journal of Personality and Social Psychology* 74, no. 2: 538–56.

Paunonen, Sampo V. 2003. "Big Five Factors of Personality and Replicated Predictions of Behavior." *Journal of Personality and Social Psychology* 84, no. 2: 411–24.

Paxton, Susan J., and Justine Diggens. 1996. "Avoidance Coping, Binge Eating, and Depression: An Examination of the Escape Theory of Binge Eating." *International Journal of Eating Disorders* 22, no. 1: 83–87.

Perera, Chandana, S. L. Kasun Dayanga, and Nisha Jayasuriya. 2013. "Factors Affecting Credit Card Debts: A Study among Executives in Sri Lanka." *International Journal of Science and Research* 5, no. 7: 1495–1504.

Pettit, Nathan C., and Niro Sivanathan. 2011. "The Plastic Trap: Self-Threat Drives Credit Usage and Status Consumption." *Social Psychological and Personality Science* 2, no. 2: 146–53.

Petit, Olivia, Frédéric Basso, Dwight Merunka, Charles Spence, Adrian David Cheok, and Olivier Oullier. 2016. "Pleasure and the Control of Food Intake: An Embodied Cognition Approach to Consumer Self-regulation." *Psychology and Marketing* 33, no. 8: 608–19.

Pham, Thi H., Keong Yap, and Nicki A. Dowling. 2012. "The Impact of Financial Management Practices and Financial Attitudes on the Relationship between Materialism and Compulsive buying." *Journal of Economic Psychology* 33, no. 3: 461–70.

Phau, Ian, and Charise Woo. 2008. "Understanding Compulsive Buying Tendencies among Young Australians." *Marketing Intelligence & Planning* 26, no. 5: 441–58.

Pinna, Federica, Bernardo Dell'Osso, Bernardo, M. Di Nicola, L. Janiri, Alfred Carlo Altamura, Bernardo Carpiniello, and Eric Hollander. 2015. "Behavioural Addictions and the Transition from DSM-IV-TR to DSM-5." *Journal of Psychopathology* 21: 380–89.

Pirog, Stephen F., and James A. Roberts. 2007. "Personality and Credit Card Misuse among College Students: The Mediating Role of Impulsiveness." *Journal of Marketing Theory and Practice* 15, no. 1: 65–77.

Piroth, Philipp, Marc Sebastian Ritter, and Edith Rueger-Muck. 2020. "Online Grocery Shopping Adoption: Do Personality Traits Matter?" *British Food Journal* 122, no. 3: 957–75.

Pradhan, Debasis, D. Israel, and Amit Kumar Jena. 2018. "Materialism and Compulsive Buying Behaviour: The Role of Consumer Credit Card Use and Impulse Buying." *Asia Pacific Journal of Marketing and Logistics* 30, no. 5: 1239–58.

Puri, Radhika. 1996. "Measuring and Modifying Consumer Impulsiveness: A Cost-Benefit Accessibility Framework." *Journal of Consumer Psychology* 5, no. 2: 87–113.

Quintelier, Ellen. 2014. "The Influence of the Big 5 Personality Traits on Young People's Political Consumer Behaviour." *Young Consumers* 15, no. 4: 342–52.

Rajamma, Rajasree K., Lou E. Pelton, Maxwell K. Hsu, and Dee K. Knight. 2010. "The Impact of Consumers' Need for Uniqueness and Nationality on Generation Y's Retail Patronage Behaviors: Investigating American and Taiwanese Consumers." *Journal of Global Marketing* 23, no. 5: 387–410.

Rajesh, Swama. 2019. "Mood Pattern for Savory and Confectionary Food Items among Gen-Y Women from Social Identity Standpoint." In Dasgupta, Sabyasachi, and Priya Grover (Eds.), *Optimizing Millennial Consumer Engagement with Mood Analysis* (pp. 118–156). Hershey, PA: IGI Global.

Raju, Puthankurissi S. 1980. "Optimum Stimulation Level: Its Relationship to Personality, Demographics, and Exploratory Behavior." *Journal of Consumer Research* 7, no. 3: 272–282.

Ramsey, Dave. 2019. "10 Ways to Stop Overspending on Impulsive Buys." Retrieved 22 July 2019, from https://www.daveramsey.com/blog/stop-impulse-buys.

Rashid, Muhammad Anwar, Talat Islam, Muhammad Uzair Malik, and Zeshan Ahmer. 2019. "Impact of Materialism on Impulsive Buying: Mediating Role of Credit Card Use and Brand Loyalty." *Pakistan Economic and Social Review* 57, no. 1: 23.

Richins, Marsha L. 2017. "Materialism Pathways: The Processes That Create and Perpetuate Materialism." *Journal of Consumer Psychology* 27, no. 4: 480–99.

Robb, Cliff A. 2011. "Financial Knowledge and Credit Card Behavior of College Students." *Journal of Family and Economic Issues* 32: 690–98.

Roberts, James A. 1998. "Compulsive Buying among College Students: An Investigation of Its Antecedents, Consequences, and Implications for Public Policy." *Journal of Consumer Affairs* 32, no. 2: 295–319.

Roberts, James A. 2000. "Consuming in a Consumer Culture: College Students, Materialism, Status Consumption, and Compulsive Buying." *Marketing Management Journal* 10, no. 2: 76–91.

Roberts, James A., and Eli Jones. 2001. "Money Attitudes, Credit Card Use, and Compulsive Buying among American College Students." *Journal of Consumer Affairs* 35, no. 2: 213–40.

Roberts, James A., and Stephen F. Pirog III. 2004. "Personal Goals and Their Role in Consumer Behavior: The Case of Compulsive Buying." *Journal of Marketing Theory and Practice* 12, no. 3: 61–73.

Roberts, James A., and Cesar J. Sepulveda M. 1999. "Money Attitudes and Compulsive Buying: An Exploratory Investigation of the Emerging Consumer Culture in Mexico." *Journal of International Consumer Marketing* 11, no. 4: 53–74.

Rohrer, Julia M., Egloff, Borris, and Stefan C. Schmukle. 2015. "Examining the Effects of Birth Order on Personality." Proceedings of the National Academy of Sciences of the United States of America, 112, 46. 14224–14229. Retrieved 25 October 2020, from https://www.pnas.org/content/112/46/14224.

Rook, Dennis W. 1987. "The Buying Impulse." *Journal of Consumer Research* 14: 189–99.

Sari, Meylisa Permata, and P. Tommy YS Suyasa, 2017. "Materialistic Value and Credit Card Usage as Predictors of Compulsive Clothing Buying among Young Adult Women." *Makara Hubs-Asia* 21, no. 2: 83–91.

Schiffman, Leon G., and Leslie L. Kanuk. 2009. *Consumer Behaviour*. Harlow, England: Prentice Hall.

Schultz, Duane P., and Sydney E. Schultz. 2017. *Theories of Personality*, 11th ed. Boston: Cengage Learning.

Shanker, Stuart. 2016. "Self-Regulation vs. Self-Control." Retrieved 28 July 2019, from https://www.psychologytoday.com/us/blog/self-reg/201607/self-reg-self-regulation-vs-self-control.

Shehzadi, Kiran, Muhammad Ahmad-ur-Rehman, Anam Mehmood Cheema, and Alishba Ahkam. 2016. "Impact of Personality Traits on Compulsive Buying Behavior: Mediating Role of Impulsive Buying." *Journal of Service Science and Management* 9, no. 5: 416–432.

Shoham, Aviv, Yossi Gavish, and Sigal Segev. 2014. "A Cross-Cultural Analysis of Impulsive and Compulsive Buying Behaviors among Israeli and U.S. Consumers: The Influence of Personal Traits and Cultural Values." *Journal of International Consumer Marketing* 27: 187–206.

Shoham, Aviv, and Maja Makovec Brenčič. 2003. "Compulsive Buying Behavior." *Journal of Consumer Marketing* 20, no. 2, 127–38.

Sidoti, Phillip M., and Raj Devasagayam. 2010. "Credit Cards and College Students: Effect of Materialism and Risk Attitude on Misuse." *The Marketing Management Journal* 20, no. 2: 64–79.

Smith, Trevor A. 2015. The Personality Trait Predictors of Brand Loyalty." *Academy of Business Research* 3: 6–21.

Smith, Trevor A. 2019. "A Buyer Behavioural Model for Associating Personality Traits with Likelihood to Buy Life Insurance." *Journal of Customer Behaviour* 18, no. 1: 61–78.

Sohn, Sang-Hee, and Yun-Jung Choi. 2012. "A Model of Compulsive Buying: Dysfunctional Beliefs and Self-regulation of Compulsive Buyers." *Social Behavior and Personality: An International Journal* 40, no. 10: 1611–24.

Soll, Jack B., Ralph L. Keeney, and Richard P. Larrick. 2013. "Consumer Misunderstanding of Credit Card Use, Payments, and Debt: Causes and Solutions." *Journal of Public Policy and Marketing* 32, no. 1: 66–81.

Solomon, Michael R. 1992. *Consumer Behavior: Buying, Having, and Being, Massachusetts*. Needham Heights, MA: Allyn and Bacon.

Soman, Dilip. 2001. "Effects of Payment Mechanism on Spending Behavior: The Role of Rehearsal and Immediacy of Payments." *Journal of Consumer Research* 27, no. 4: 460–74.

Srivastava, Utkarsh, and Santosh Gopalkrishnan. 2015. "Impact of Big Data Analytics on the Banking Sector: Learning for Indian Banks." *Procedia Computer Science* 50: 643–52.

Stadler, William A. 2012. "Predatory Lending: Is the Credit Card Act Enough?" *Journal of Financial Crime* 19, no. 1: 99–111.

Stanton, Steven J., Walter Sinnott-Armstrong, and Scott A. Huettel. 2017. "Neuromarketing: Ethical Implications of Its Use and Potential Misuse." *Journal of Business Ethics* 144, no. 4: 799–811.

Steele, Jason. 2018. "The History of Credit Cards." *Experian*. Retrieved 25 November 2020, from https://www.experian.com/blogs/ask-experian/the-history-of-credit-cards/.

Steenkamp, Jan-Benedict E. M., and Alberto Maydeu-Olivares. 2015. "Stability and Change in Consumer Traits: Evidence from a 12-year Longitudinal Study 2002–2013." *Journal of Marketing Research* 52, no. 3: 287–308.

Stoll, Mary Lyn. 2002. "The Ethics of Marketing Good Corporate Conduct." *Journal of Business Ethics* 41, nos. 1–2: 121–29.

Sultan, Abdullah J., Jeff Joireman, and David E. Sprott. 2012. "Building Consumer Self-Control: The Effect of Self-Control Exercises on Impulse Buying Urges." *Marketing Letters* 23, no. 1: 61–72.

Swift, Art, and Steve Ander. 2016. "Most Americans See the Death of Cash in Their Lifetime. *Gallup Marketplace*. Retrieved 25 November 2020, from https://news.gallup.com/poll/193706/americans-foresee-death-cash-lifetime.aspx.

Thompson, Edmund R., and Gerard P. Prendergast. 2015. "The Influence of Trait Affect and the Five-Factor Personality Model on Impulse Buying." *Personality and Individual Differences* 76: 216–21.

Thornquist, Clemens. 2017. "Unemotional Design: An Alternative Approach to Sustainable Design." *Design Issues* 33, no. 4: 83–91.

Tian, Kelly Tepper, William O. Bearden, and Gary L. Hunter. 2001. "Consumers' Need for Uniqueness: Scale Development and Validation." *Journal of Consumer Research* 28, no. 1: 50–66.

Valence, Gilles, Alain d'Astous, and Louis Fortier. 1988. "Compulsive Buying: Concept and Measurement." *Journal of Consumer Policy* 11, no. 4: 419–33.

Veblen, Thorstein. 1918. *The Theory of the Leisure Class: An Economic Study of Institutions*. New York: B. W. Huebsch.

Veludo-de-Oliveira, Tania Modesto, Marcelo Augusto Falciano, and Renato Villas Boas Perito. 2014. "Effects of Credit Card Usage on Young Brazilians' Compulsive Buying." *Young Consumers Insight and Ideas for Responsible Marketers* 15, no. 5: 111–24.

Verplanken, Bas, and Astrid Herabadi. 2001. "Individual Differences in Impulse Buying Tendency: Feeling and No Thinking." *European Journal of Personality* 15, S1: S71–S83.

Verplanken, Bas, and Ayana Sato. 2011. "The Psychology of Impulse Buying: An Integrative Self-Regulation Approach." *Journal of Consumer Policy* 34, no. 2: 197–210.

Vohs, Kathleen D., and Roy F. Baumeister, (Eds.). 2016. *Handbook of Self-Regulation: Research, Theory, and Applications*. New York: Guilford Publications.

Vohs, Kathleen D., Roy F. Baumeister, Brandon J. Schmeichel, Jean M. Twenge, Noelle M. Nelson, and Dianne M. Tice. 2008a. "Making Choices Impairs Subsequent Self-Control: A Limited-Resource Account of Decision Making, Self-Regulation, and Active Initiative." *Journal of Personality and Social Psychology* 94: 883–98.

Vohs, Kathleen D., Roy F. Baumeister, and Diane M. Tice. 2008b. "Self-Regulation: Goals, Gonsumption, and Choices." In Haugtvedt, Curtis P., Paul M. Herr, and Frank R. Kardes (Eds.), *Marketing and Consumer Psychology Series: Vol. 4. Handbook of Consumer Psychology* (pp. 349–366). London: Taylor & Francis Group/Lawrence Erlbaum Associates.

Vohs, Kathleen, and Ronald Faber. 2003. "Self-Regulation and Impulsive Spending Patterns." In Keller, Punam Anand, and Dennis W. Rook (Eds.), *NA—Advances in Consumer Research*, vol. 30 (pp. 125–26). Valdosta, GA: Association for Consumer Research.

Weinstein, Aviv, Aniko Maraz, Mark D. Griffiths, Michel Lejoyeux, and Zsolt Demetrovics. 2016. "Compulsive Buying—Features and Characteristics of Addiction." In *Neuropathology of Drug Addictions and Substance Misuse* (pp. 993–1007). Cambridge, MA: Academic Press.

Wharton. 2003. "What Women Buy—and Why." Retrieved 19 November 2020, from https://knowledge.wharton.upenn.edu/article/what-women-buy-and-why/.

White, Michelle J. 2007. "Bankruptcy Reform and Credit Cards." *Journal of Economic Perspectives* 21, no. 4: 175–99.

Williams, Monnica T., Beth Mugno, Martin Franklin, and Sonya Faber. 2013. "Symptom Dimensions in Obsessive-Compulsive Disorder: Phenomenology and Treatment Outcomes with Exposure and Ritual Prevention." *Psychopathology* 46: 365–76.

Wolfinbarger, Mary, and Mary C. Gilly. 2001. "Shopping Online for Freedom, Control, and Fun." *California Management Review* 43, no. 2: 34–55.

Wolters, Timothy. 2000. "'Carry Your Credit in Your Pocket': The Early History of the Credit Card at Bank of America and Chase Manhattan." *Enterprise & Society* 1: 315–54.

Woo, Hyunhee, and Hyung Jun Ahn. 2015. "Big Five Personality and Different Meanings of Happiness of Consumers." *Economics and Sociology* 8, no. 3: 145–54.

Workman, Leity, and David Paper. 2010. "Compulsive Buying: A Theoretical Framework." *The Journal of Business Inquiry* 9, no. 1: 89–126.

Worthy, Sheri Lokken, Jeffrey Jonkman, and Lynn Blinn-Pike. 2010. "Sensation-Seeking, Risk-Taking, and Problematic Financial Behaviors of College Students." *Journal of Family and Economic Issues* 31, no. 2: 161–70.

Xiao, Jing Jian, Chuanyi Tang, Joyce Serido, and Soyeon Shim. 2011. "Antecedents and Consequences of Risky Credit Behavior among College Students: Application and Extension of the Theory of Planned Behavior." *Journal of Public Policy & Marketing* 30, no. 2: 239–45.

Xu, Haiqin, Kem ZK Zhang, and Sesia J. Zhao. 2020. "A Dual Systems Model of Online Impulse Buying." *Industrial Management & Data Systems* 120, no. 5: 845–61.

Yamauchi, Kent T., and Donald J. Templer. 1982. "The Development of a Money Attitude Scale." *Journal of Personality Assessment* 46, no. 5: 522–28.

Yurchisin, Jennifer, and Kim K. P. Johnson. 2004. "Compulsive Buying Behavior and Its Relationship to Perceived Social Status Associated with Buying, Materialism, Self-Esteem, and Apparel-Product Involvement." *Family and Consumer Sciences Research Journal* 32, no. 3: 291–314.

Zainudin, Rozaimah, Nurul Shahnaz Mahdzan, and Ming-Yee Yeap. 2019. "Determinants of Credit Card Misuse among Gen Y Consumers in Urban Malaysia." *International Journal of Bank Marketing* 37, no. 5: 1350–70.

Zhao, Yi, Ying Zhao, and Inseong Song. 2009. "Predicting New Customers' Risk Type in the Credit Card Market." *Journal of Marketing Research* 46, no. 4: 506–17.

Zadka, Łukasz, and Marcin Olajossy. 2016. "Compulsive Buying in Outline." *Psychiatria Polska* 50, no. 1: 153–64.

Zaharie, Monica Maria, and Andreea Ioana Maniu. 2012. "How Could Children Become Bad Consumers-Materialistic Values and Ethics." In *The Proceedings of the International Conference Marketing—from Information to Decision* (p. 515). Babes Bolyai University.

Index

About the Authors

Trevor A. Smith is a senior lecturer in marketing and research methods at Mona School of Business and Management, University of the West Indies. He has published in several rated international journals in research streams including marketing, consumer psychology and business. Dr. Smith is a general research methodologist who utilizes structural equations modelling in most of his work. He has served in management and board directorship capacities in a number of private and public sector organizations in Jamaica and currently serves as chairman of the National Conservation Trust Fund of Jamaica. He is the holder of a doctorate in business administration (Nova Southeastern University, USA), a master's in business administration (Barry University, USA) and a bachelor of science honours degree with double majors in mathematics and computer science (University of the West Indies, Mona Campus).

Kenroy C. Wedderburn is an associate professor of finance at Concord University—a state university in West Virginia, USA. Prior to that he was an associate professor and associate dean of the School of Business at Wayland Baptist University in Texas, USA. Before that he worked in both the private and public sectors in Jamaica while being an adjunct professor for several years. Dr. Wedderburn was a CEO of a public sector agency, and prior to that spent eight years as a senior manager at an international bank—The Bank of Nova Scotia (with headquarters in Canada). He holds a doctorate in business administration (Nova Southeastern University), an MBA in finance (Pace University) and a bachelor's degree with double major in computer science and management. He additionally holds the CFP® (Certified Financial Planner) certification and the AAPA (Associate, Annuity Products and Administration).